GREAT MYSTERIES

JOHN GRANT

THE
APPLE
PRESS

DEDICATION

To Jenny Randles, with affection and respect

A QUINTET BOOK

Published by Apple Press Ltd.
6 Blundell Street
London, N7 9BH

ISBN 1-85076-143-4

This book was designed and produced by
Quintet Publishing Limited
6 Blundell Street
London N7 9BH

Design Director: Peter Bridgewater
Art Director: Ian Hunt
Designer: Annie Moss
Editors: Caroline Beattie, Judith Simons
Picture Research: Anne-Marie Ehrlich

Typeset in Great Britain by
Context Typesetting, Brighton
Manufactured in Hong Kong by
Regent Publishing Services Limited
Printed in Hong Kong by
South Sea Int'l Press Ltd.

CONTENTS

INTRODUCTION
IS SEEING BELIEVING?

 THERE IS AN OLD Chinese curse: 'May you live through interesting times.'

Whether we regard ourselves as cursed or not, there can hardly be any question that the times we live in are interesting. To look on the dark side, wars and human greed conspire to ensure that all too many of us die through violence or through starvation. On the other hand, most readers of this book will remember the magical moment when, for the first time, a human being walked on the surface of the moon. The Soviet Union is planning to send people to Mars before the end of the century. All over the world, genetic engineers claim that their discoveries will soon be able to obviate hereditary mental retardation, crop failures and many other of the evils that beset humanity. Computer scientists – notably in Japan – predict that within the next decade or so they will be able to construct computers as intelligent and creative as human beings.

These are indeed interesting times.

One of the ways in which they are interesting is that our worldview is in a state' of flux. For untold centuries our ancestors were eagerly credulous, believing implicitly in each new 'marvel'. Then science came along, and for the past couple of centuries intelligent people believed only in phenomena that could be reproduced in the laboratory – or, in the case of astronomy, observed by all and sundry.

During this century, things have changed. A number of scientists have realized that there are some things which current science is incapable of explaining, that it is no longer possible to dismiss *all* sightings of UFOs or reports of poltergeists as silly-season stories. It is necessary to examine such events, to reveal them as hoaxes or misinterpretations if that is indeed the case, and to investigate the ones left over – the ones that are, in every sense of the word, mysteries.

This book is in two parts. The first is concerned with mysteries that seem certainly connected with the human mind and body; the second deals with 'external' phenomena, such as UFOs and the Yeti. In a way, this differentiation is artificial, because we have no real reason to believe that many if not all of the 'external' phenomena are not likewise products of the human mind.

Before we examine these mysteries, there are a couple of things we must bear in mind. The first is the 'improbability law'. This has been derived empirically, and states the following: in the field of mysteries, the more apparently ridiculous a phenomenon is, the more likely it is to be genuine. The corollary is that, if a particular paranormal power or event is, as it were, 'socially acceptable', then we should view it with some suspicion. It is as if the intuition of our intellects (to coin an apparent contradiction in terms) is profoundly unreliable when it comes to examining the paranormal. In a rather different context, Arthur C Clarke came close to this when he produced his famous First Law: 'When a distinguished but elderly scientist states that something is possible, he is almost certainly right. When he states that something is impossible, he is very probably wrong.'

It would seem that our intellects are like a 'distinguished but elderly scientist', dismissing out of hand everything that does not fit in with a strictly rationalist world-view. In many cases, of course, this 'scientist' is quite right: pigs do not fly. But when it comes to the paranormal the 'scientist' makes grave errors of judgement, which possibly give us a clue as to the nature of mysteries. It is our intellect – the 'scientist' inside each one of us – that tells us what is probable and what is not. If other people see a shower of hazelnuts fall inexplicably from the sky, all our intellect can do is look at the hazelnuts; it rejects the testimony of the observers. Yet our intellect is not doing so for any properly scientific reason; it is perfectly possible that the laws of nature are such that every now and then the sky precipitates hazelnuts. We just do not know – and so automatic intellectual rejection of the notion is highly unscientific. There may be a perfectly rationalist explanation of such phenomena, fitting in happily with the ideas of modern science. It may be that the mystery has been born from the imaginations of hoaxers (although it is hard to picture people staggering around with sacks of hazelnuts just to get their pictures in the local newspaper); but equally it may be that there are some things about this world and this universe about which we understand absolutely nothing.

This is not just an unhelpful 'there are more things in heaven and earth' comment. Obviously, there is an infinitude of things which science does not yet know – there have been scientific proofs that we can *never* know everything; yet science has roughed out a very good picture of the way that nature behaves, even if it will be forever incapable of painting in the details. What we are referring to are images that do not even appear in the picture – laws of which we have not even the slightest inkling.

ABOVE: *"Gnome" with Elsie Wright, photographed by Frances Griffiths at Cottingley Glen, West Yorkshire (England), in September 1917.*

It is, perhaps, precisely because we have not the faintest notion of such natural activities that the 'improbability law' comes into play. A shower of hazelnuts is an affront to our intellects because whatever brought it about is totally outside our current scientific knowledge. If we had even a smidgeon of understanding of what was going on, then the event would no longer be a mystery; instead, it would be a subject for scientific examination.

It is worth bearing in mind the 'improbability law' as we examine the various mysteries discussed in this book. A second factor to remember is the divided brain.

Split-brain research has revealed that there are, in essence, two 'people' living inside each of us. One of the people is the conscious 'you', which is generally sited in the left hemisphere of the brain. The 'you', or left-brain, is good with words, is rational and logical, and can be regarded as the intellectual side of the composite person each of us is. The right-brain, by contrast, is generally silent, although on occasion it makes its presence felt – in dreams, for example, or when we have hunches. Freud came close to describing the 'person' resident in the right-brain when he developed his idea of the unconscious.

The right-brain is not good at logic – at least, not logic as understood by the left-brain. The right-brain, therefore, is incapable of distinguishing between events which the left-brain categorizes as either 'probable' or 'improbable': so far as the right-brain is concerned, things either happen or they do not. The left-brain is pretty certain that the sun will rise tomorrow; the right-brain regards each dawn as something fresh and new.

Too many paranormal theorists have gone overboard about this. They say that the right-brain is capable of ranging through time, throwing heavy objects about, and so on, and then they sit back, satisfied, as if this provided some sort of total explanation. Of course, it does not. Assuming that the right-brain has these abilities, we still do not know *how* it can do these things.

Nevertheless, we can say with some degree of certainty that the right-brain is involved in most paranormal events – certainly in those described in the first part of this book, and possibly in most of those described in the second. Ignoring for the moment all the other evidence that this is the case, we can simply note that the 'improbability law' fits in so perfectly with our ideas about the patterns of right-brain thinking that it is hard to believe that it can be a mere coincidence.

Clearly we must be cautious as we approach the mysteries described in this book: we must keep both our gullibility and our scepticism in check as we evaluate the evidence before us. We must remember that the camera can lie – as, all too easily, can human beings! – but at the same time we must remember that our conscious, intellectual, left-brain self is a 'distinguished but elderly scientist' whose preconceptions and received notions may make him or her a poor judge of the evidence.

Care has been taken over the selection of mysteries to be discussed in this book. Famous 'mysteries' that have proved to be anything but are referred to only in passing – the case of the *Mary Celeste* is one such. Instead, the concentration is upon those events and phenomena that are particularly revealing, either because they are typical of a whole range of similar mysteries or because they are so far outside the normal limits of our understanding that they have a specific interest for exactly that reason.

One final caution. It may well be that, one day, you will find yourself in direct contact with a 'mystery'. Beware of accepting it too easily. That UFO you see could easily be a high-flying aircraft; the person who can bend cutlery using 'psychic' means may be only a conjurer. Never on any account part with any money if someone claims that he can contact your deceased sister or transport you to the planet Venus. Retain your scepticism at all times: 99 per cent of all apparent mysteries can be explained in rationalist terms, often quite easily.

On the other hand, the remaining one per cent cannot. These represent the true mysteries.

PART ONE

MYSTERIES
OF
MIND AND BODY

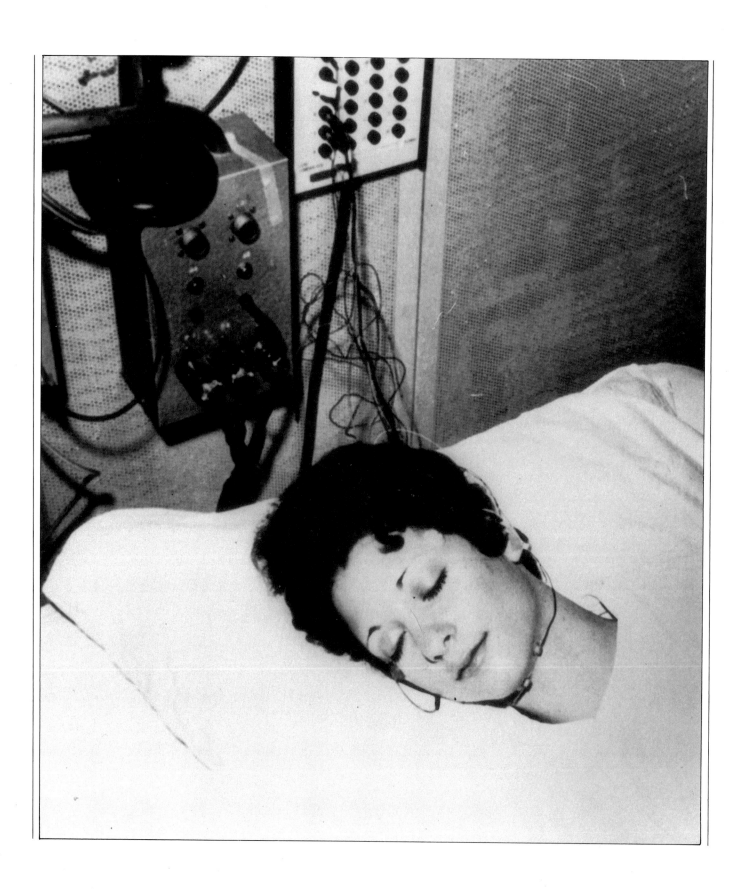

TELEPATHY

IN THE 1950s A small boy at a Scottish school discovered that he had forgotten his school-lunch ticket. He walked home to see if his mother were in. She was not, but, just as he was about to turn hungrily and disconsolately away, she appeared in the distance. She had been lunching in the university staff canteen nearby and had suddenly 'realized' that her son was at the family home and needed her. The 'message' had been strong enough for her to break off her lunch, say goodbye to her colleagues, and walk to the house.

Telepathy? It would seem so. Most people have had an experience of this sort at some time during their lives. Of course, in this instance it might simply have been that the mother unconsciously remembered that she had failed to give her son a lunch ticket, but such plausible explanations are far from frequently available. Many families are familiar with the phenomenon that, when one of them is in trouble, no matter how far away, the others somehow 'know'.

This sort of everyday telepathy is frequently reported, especially between family members, lovers and twins. However, formal experiments on telepathy have produced precious little by way of hard evidence. Normally cited are the experiments of J B and L E Rhine, which would seem to provide powerful evidence in favour of telepathy. Unfortunately, one cannot take these experiments at face value: the scientific controls used by the Rhines, while they improved over the years, were never better than slack. An

*The husband-and-wife team of Professor J B **ABOVE** and Dr L E Rhine **RIGHT** did pioneering work to investigate the phenomenon of telepathy. Their experiments produced some interesting results, but in recent years concern has been voiced about their methodology. **LEFT** An experiment underway on dream telepathy in the famous Maimonides Medical Center, Brooklyn, New York. The sleeping subject is wired up to an EEG (electroencephalogram) and a polygraph.*

while Linzmayer sat in the back, having been firmly instructed not to look! As soon as more rigorous scientific controls were introduced Linzmayer's paranormal abilities curiously declined.

Yet telepathic experiences between people emotionally close are common, as we have noted. Rather like the example cited above was an experience had by the noted medium Eileen Garrett, who was born in Ireland but lived for much of her life in the United States. While living in London she had a curious dream about her daughter, who was away at boarding school. The daughter appeared in the dream, apologizing for the fact that she had not written the standard weekly letter home. She was suffering from some kind of chest fever and really was not up to the effort. The headmistress had initially berated her for failing to write, but now, seeing how ill she was, was being sympathetic. Sure enough, the weekly letter failed to arrive, and so Garrett telephoned the school. She spoke with the headmistress and discovered that indeed her daughter was in bed with a bad chest cold and had used this as an excuse, justified or otherwise, for declining to write home.

Oddly enough, while Garrett had various 'classic' telepathic experiences like this one, as soon as she went into the laboratory at Maimonides for testing by Ullman and Krippner her results became far less convincing. There are two possible reasons for this. Either she was vastly exaggerating the degree of coincidence between

early example will suffice. A 'psychic', A J Linzmayer, was tested early on by J B Rhine, and his rate of success when guessing the cards turned up by Rhine was astonishing; the odds against its having happened by chance were approximately 17 thousand million to one. Alas, these odds shorten quite a lot when the circumstances of the experiments are taken into account. In some, Rhine sat in the front of his car

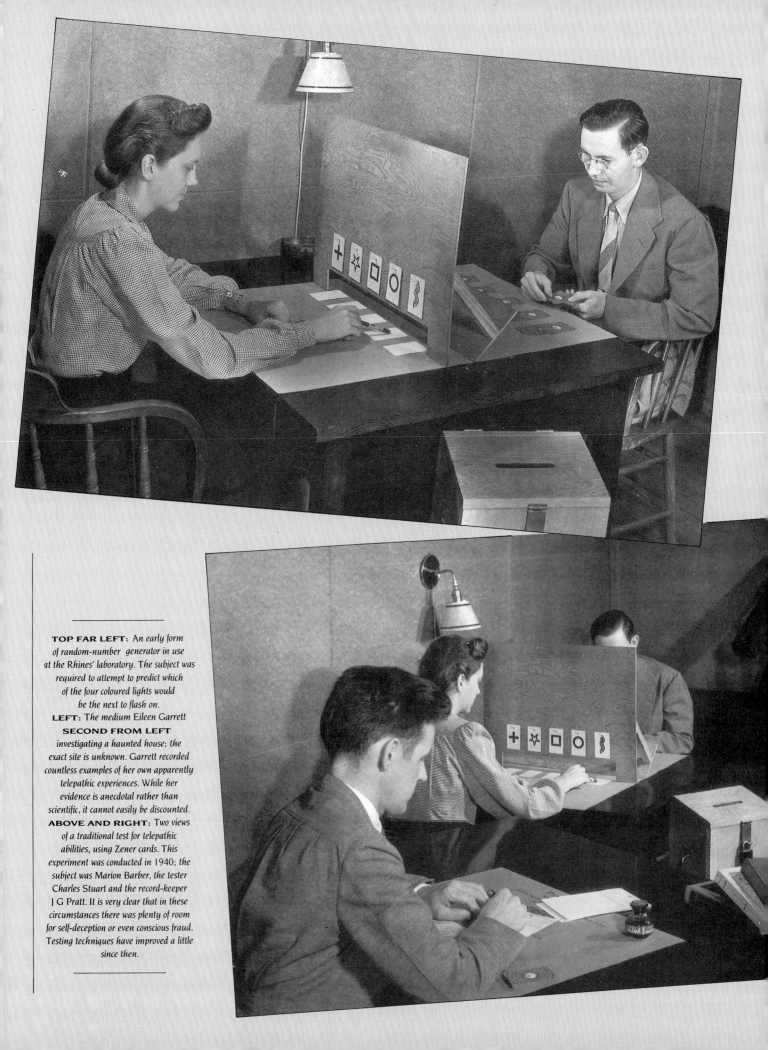

TOP FAR LEFT: An early form of random-number generator in use at the Rhines' laboratory. The subject was required to attempt to predict which of the four coloured lights would be the next to flash on.

LEFT: The medium Eileen Garrett **SECOND FROM LEFT** investigating a haunted house; the exact site is unknown. Garrett recorded countless examples of her own apparently telepathic experiences. While her evidence is anecdotal rather than scientific, it cannot easily be discounted.

ABOVE AND RIGHT: Two views of a traditional test for telepathic abilities, using Zener cards. This experiment was conducted in 1940; the subject was Marion Barber, the tester Charles Stuart and the record-keeper J G Pratt. It is very clear that in these circumstances there was plenty of room for self-deception or even conscious fraud. Testing techniques have improved a little since then.

her telepathic 'visions' and the reality, or – as has so often been claimed – whatever it is that is responsible for the paranormal declines to perform in a laboratory environment. (A third possibility is that as soon as people start to *try* to have paranormal experiences they find it impossible.)

Another astonishing example of telepathic dreaming was reported in 1884 by a Mrs Philip Crellin. She reported that

three weeks ago, I was unable to sleep during the early hours of the night. I thought, amongst other things, of a rather comic piece of poetry which my husband used to repeat years ago I stuck at one line and could not recall it. However, I fell asleep, and three or four hours after awoke, to find it was time to rise. My husband, after a good night's rest . . . awoke also; he stretched out his hand towards me, and repeated the line I had failed to remember in the night, and which did not occupy my thoughts when I awoke in the morning.

It is conceivable that Mrs Crellin talked in her sleep, which might explain her husband's apparent telepathy, but this is rendered less than likely by the sheer volume of similar cases of sleeping spouses 'picking up' the thoughts of their awake partners. To quote just one more example, dating from about the same time as Mrs Crellin's experience, a certain Mrs Jean Fielding was lying awake while her husband snored and suddenly thought for the first time in years of a man called Harvey Brown, who had lived near to her girlhood home and who had been a very peripheral acquaintance. In the morning her husband mentioned that he had had a strange dream about this very same Harvey Brown.

Could such cases as these be merely coincidence? Possibly yes, but so many have been reported that it requires little knowledge of statistics to realize that the odds against pure coincidence are huge. However, we should be careful about the use of statistics by some paranormal investigators. Often you will read, for example, that an experimentee's ability to 'read' cards must be telepathic, because the odds against his or her 'hit rate' are so enormous. Sometimes, though, these vast odds are a result not of psychic powers but simply of the experimental technique. Imagine a card-reading experiment which starts off with 100 volunteers. After the first round of experiments the 50 lowest scores are discarded, and attention is focused on the others. The process is repeated until only a single individual is left – whose scores, not surprisingly, fly right in

the face of the statistical odds. In this kind of experiment, there will obviously always be such an individual.

However, some statistical results provide genuine evidence in favour of the existence of telepathy. In 1942 Dr Gertrude Schmeidler performed a famous experiment. A group of volunteers were asked to 'read' cards. Before the experiment started she asked the people to declare whether they believed in the existence of telepathy; the sceptics she dubbed the 'goats' and the believers the 'sheep'. The 'sheep' produced results better than those to be expected through coincidence, but even more interesting was that the 'goats' produced significantly worse results. One possible explanation is that the left-brains of the sceptics overrode their right-brains; another possibility is that the 'sheep' believed in telepathy because they had already experienced it.

Many people – and possibly most – believe in telepathy, but the evidence is ambiguous, and certainly not as good as that in favour of some rather more outré 'mysteries' . . . as we shall see.

TOP: *Gertrude Schmeidler, the researcher who conducted the famous 'sheep and goats' experiment, one of the most significant in the history of research into ESP. The 'sheep' (believers) scored notably better than would have statistically been expected but, even more importantly, the scores of the 'goats' (non-believers) were substantially worse than they should have been had mere chance been involved.*

PRECOGNITION

THERE ARE TWO WAYS of viewing precognition, the ability to detect or predict future events. One is that certain people are, quite simply, able to have sight of events that have not yet occurred. The other, by far the more controversial, is that our right-brains are capable of making minor modifications to the present and accurately foreseeing the more major future consequences of those changes. Both hypotheses are, of course, impossible to prove or disprove, and the same has to be said of the whole phenomenon of precognition itself, although the anecdotal evidence is overwhelming.

Precognition must be thought of in conjunction with the topic of coincidence. Imagine that you have the impression that you will be kicked by a horse tomorrow. If, as is very likely, you fail to be kicked by a horse, you will forget your foreboding. But if you are indeed kicked by a horse you will tell the world of your 'precognitive' experience. In other words, we remember coincidences but we are never aware of 'non-coincidences'. We must bear in mind, therefore, that a large part of the evidence for apparent precognition is necessarily explicable in terms of pure coincidence.

This argument can be turned on its head. Perhaps a lot of the things we regard as coincidences are in fact paranormal events. This was an idea that appealed to the psychoanalyst C G Jung, who produced a theory, 'synchronicity', to explain coincidences. The details are complex, but the overall notion was that there is some 'acausal principle' that operates in such a way that coincidental events occur that seem to *us* to have no causal link. By way of analogy, a fly sitting on the minute-hand of a clock might think it a strange coincidence that, every time the hand was vertical, bells started chiming; as far as the fly is concerned, there is an 'acausal principle' at work.

Jung, like the Austrian biologist Paul Kammerer, 'collected' coincidences. In a famous example, he noted one day that the number of his streetcar was the same as that of the ticket he had bought for the theatre the same evening; and he was surprised to find the number turning up during a telephone conversation he had that same day. The American psychic Alan Vaughan, not long after reading of this, was thinking about Jung's experience and looked at his own streetcar-ticket number: it was 096960, a number which can be read identically upside-down. On leaving the streetcar, he noticed that its number, too, was one that read the same when upside-down. Eagerly looking around for further examples of such synchronicity, he almost fell over an ashcan. Imagine his astonishment when he saw the name painted on it: JUNG!

A great deal of precognition comes about through dreams. However, some examples occur not just while the predictor is conscious but through a deliberate effort of will. Colin Wilson has cited the instance of a psychic named Orlop who, asked by the Israeli Parapsychological Society to give details of the occupant of a specific chair at one of their meetings some weeks hence, did so with a fair degree of accuracy. Kevin McClure, then of the Oxford University Society for Psychical Research, repeated the experiment, the psychic on this occasion being Robert Cracknell, and once again the results were far better than anything that could be explained away as coincidence. Psychic detective Gerard Croiset has likewise had a fair degree of success in such trials.

ABOVE: *Gerard Croiset, the celebrated psychic detective. In some cases his results have been astonishingly successful; in others they have been the exact opposite.*

To describe these experiments as 'controlled' would be to overstate matters; nevertheless it is hard to find any other explanation for them than that the phenomenon of precognition genuinely exists. Here, of course, our 'model' of precognition – that it is not so much that people predict the future, more that their right-brains act in such a way as to mould it – runs into a number of problems. It is very hard to see how the right-brain of either Orlop or Cracknell could have 'arranged' for a particular stranger to be in a particular place at a particular time. This may well be a fault in the 'model'; equally, it may be that the right-brain is capable of operating with a subtlety incomprehensible to the conscious left-brain.

Some people have made international reputations out of their supposed precognitive abilities. Notable among these are the so-called 'psychic detectives', such as Croiset, Cracknell and Peter Hurkos. These people have claimed the ability to handle objects and thereby detect their histories (an ability technically termed 'psychometry'). It is hard to establish the success rate of such enterprises, but some of the results have been startling, to say the least. For example, when Peter Hurkos was called in to help in the investigation of the Boston Strangler case, he handled the clothing of some of the victims and then gave very precise details of the person responsible for the killings. His predictions, which included bizarre personal habits, were absolutely spot-on, right down to the address – but the individual concerned was only a minor sex offender, not the murderer.

How did this come about? There is no real reason to believe that the relevant underwear had been handled by the sex offender (although Hurkos himself wonders if there was a miscarriage of justice). It seems possible that what Hurkos did was to predict the arrest of the fetishist and the discovery of the objects he had collected. If so, Hurkos' contact with the underwear may have sparked off something rather different to psychometry: it may have concentrated his right-brain on the subject of fetishism, with the result that it was able to forecast the arrest of a particular sex offender – which arrest, of course, it actually *caused*.

Any sensible discussion of precognition must take account of our current scientific understanding of the nature of time. This differs quite substantially from the popular notion of time, which suggests that it simply 'flows'. Time to the scientist is a dimension, to be considered alongside the dimensions of length, width and depth. We can manipulate events within the three common dimensions; so it seems

feasible that we can also manipulate things within the fourth.

Also we view time as being an *ordering* of events: the past precedes the present which precedes the future. We talk of the 'arrow of time' and assume that it can never do otherwise. Yet this is not necessarily the case. For example, if there are in distant parts of the universe galaxies made up of antimatter, rather than matter, then according to some scientists the 'arrow of time' there must point in the opposite 'direction'.

Finally we must remember tachyons. It is often stated that Einstein's theory of relativity says that nothing can travel faster than the speed of light. This is an erroneous simplification. The implication of relativity is that nothing material can travel *at* the speed of light. The mathematics of relativity allows for particles that *always* travel faster than light – and, indeed, cannot be slowed down to sub-light velocities. If tachyons exist, and there is some reason to believe they do, then the mathematics is such that they must be travelling 'backwards' in time.

Time is, then, not quite the simple thing we perceive it to be. If, as science suggests, time can do things like run 'backwards', scientists must accept that precognition is a very real possibility. Whether people capable of it are, as it were, unconscious tachyon-detectors, or whether their right-brains are capable of manipulating the future – or whether there is some totally different explanation – is something about which we can, at this stage, only guess. However, the weight of evidence – anecdotal and bitty although it may be – is currently in favour of precognition.

PARANORMAL DREAMING

SAMUEL CLEMENS HAD A curiously frightening dream in 1858, when he was 23, long before he became famous as Mark Twain. At the time, he and his brother, Henry, were making a living working on the Mississippi riverboats. In his dream Samuel saw his brother's body laid out in the family living-room in a metal coffin supported between two chairs; a bouquet of white flowers, with a single red flower in the centre, lay on the corpse's breast. The dream so affected Samuel that when he awoke he told his sister that it was his sincere belief that Henry was dead.

In fact, Henry proved still to be very much alive. But some weeks later Henry was one of many people killed when the boiler of the boat on which he was working exploded. His remains were rescued and, thanks to the ladies of Memphis, who took pity on his youth and made a collection, were laid out in an expensive metal coffin, rather than a cheap wooden one, as with all the other victims of the tragedy. Samuel's first sight of his brother's body reflected precisely the scene of his dream – except for the fact that it was in someone else's living-room and that there was no bouquet of flowers on Henry's chest. Just then, however, a woman entered the room and placed a wreath of white flowers, with a red one at the centre, exactly where Samuel had seen it in his dream.

This startling account of precognitive dreaming is widely reported. But is the story in fact true? The sole source is Twain's *Autobiography*, which actually consists of a chaotic collection of disjointed ramblings, most of them taken down by friends to his dictation. One of those friends frankly described much of the contents as straight fiction. So the story may have been nothing more than a 'good tale' devised by Twain in his senility. It *might* be true, but we have no way of telling.

This is a not infrequent conclusion when studying records of paranormal dreams. There are several reasons for this. One is that people often simply lie, pretending in the aftermath of a real event that they dreamed about it beforehand.

Far more subtle – and far harder to detect because there is no deliberate deceit involved – is 'reading back'. Imagine that you dreamed one night that you were flying, and the next day you fell down the stairs – in other words, 'flew'. There is a similarity between the dream and the reality, enough of a similarity that you will very likely 'misremember' your dream, your unconscious mind altering its memories of the dream until the details tally in full detail with the reality.

It is worth stressing that 'reading back' is not a conscious effect; it will happen unless you take steps to avoid it (such as keeping a dream diary). The phenomenon makes life difficult for researchers because the dreamer is quite genuinely convinced that his or her dream accurately foretold the future.

TOP LEFT: *Peter Hurkos, like Croiset a psychic detective, played a notable part in the famous Boston Strangler case. Although he was unable to identify the murderer (Albert de Salvo), his results were so curious that they cannot be coincidental.*

RIGHT: *Samuel Clemens ('Mark Twain') who in later life claimed to have had a precognitive dream about the tragic death of his brother.*

A third difficulty in evaluating paranormal dreams is that 'the story improves with the telling'. For example, we read that Cicero once dreamed that he saw a youth being lowered on a golden chain from the skies to stand in a temple door. The next morning he was introduced by Julius Caesar to the youth of his dream – Gaius Octavius, who was later to become Augustus, Rome's first emperor. Indeed, Augustus was responsible for having Cicero put to death, and our first account of this dream dates from a time some while after this event. It seems almost certainly to have been a tale which was concocted by later historians. The dreams interpreted by Joseph in *Genesis XII* are probably a product of similar inventiveness by chroniclers (although there was indeed an important seer, possibly called Joseph, in Egypt at that time).

LEFT: *A bust of Cicero, who was widely reported to have had a precognitive dream identifying the future Emperor Augustus . However, the first account of this dates from some while after the accession of Augustus and the death of Cicero, so there is every reason to be sceptical about the story.* **ABOVE**: *One of many contemporary prints showing the failed actor John Wilkes Booth assassinating Abraham Lincoln in 1865. Thirty years later Ward Hill Lamon would recount how the president had dreamed of his forthcoming assassination.*

This urge to embellish a good tale causes investigators problems even when dealing with events as recent as the 19th century. One of the most famous precognitive dreams was recounted by Abraham Lincoln to a circle of friends in April, 1865. Lincoln dreamed that he was in bed at the White House when he heard the sounds of mourning filling the air. He got out of bed and went to find out what was going on.

> . . . I kept on until I arrived at the East Room, which I entered. There I met with a sickening surprise. Before me was a catafalque, on which rested a corpse wrapped in funeral vestments. Around it were stationed soldiers who were acting as guards; and there was a throng of people, some gazing mournfully upon the corpse, whose face was covered, others weeping pitifully. 'Who is dead in the White House?' I demanded of one of the soldiers. 'The President,' was his answer; 'he was killed by an assassin!'

Unfortunately, the details of the dream were not noted down at the time. The first written version of it appeared in 1895 in *Recollections of Lincoln* by Ward Hill Lamon, one of the company to whom Lincoln had recounted the dream. Why, one wonders, did Lamon not tell the world about it the moment Lincoln was assassinated? The answer is depressingly obvious.

Even if the tale is true, it hardly stands as a great example of precognitive dreaming, because Lincoln was anyway much concerned about the danger of being assassinated. This comment, however, does not apply to some dreams about other assassinations. About ten days before the murder of the British prime minister, Spencer Perceval, in 1812 a banker called John Williams dreamed that he was in the lobby of the House of Commons when he saw 'a small man, dressed in a blue coat and white waistcoat', whom he was told was Perceval. Williams saw this person shot dead by a man in a 'snuff-coloured coat with metal buttons'. Williams awoke and told his wife about the dream; she told him not to be so silly and to go back to sleep – which he did, only to experience the same dream twice more. Over the next day or two he told several people about the dreams, which had affected him considerably. It was only two days after Perceval's death that Williams heard about the murder. Even then, he seems not to have been overly impressed until, some weeks later, he was in London and came across a cheap drawing of the dramatic scene: all the details were exactly as in his dream, notably the clothing worn by Perceval and his murderer, John Bellingham.

There are two important points here. First, Williams told a number of people about the dreams, and later they willingly substantiated his account. Second, living far from London, Williams had little clue as to whom his dream referred – he thought of Perceval as chancellor of the exchequer, little realizing that he was prime minister, too – and so it would have been difficult for him to invent the details. It is possible that the description of the clothing is a product of unconscious 'reading back' on seeing the cheap drawing, but the overall burden of the dream cannot be so easily discounted. There is every reason to believe that this was a genuine precognitive dream.

The most famous assassinations of this century are probably those of John and Robert Kennedy. In the aftermath of both murders, people all over the world claimed to have 'previewed' the killings. The best known claimant is Jeane Dixon; unfortunately, her story does not stand up to rigorous investigation. Rather more interesting is a dream had by the American seer Alan Vaughan which seemed to predict the assassination of Robert Kennedy. The dream is

interesting for both its similarities to and differences from the actuality. The circumstantial details are strikingly similar in both dream and reality (Vaughan kept a dream diary, so that we know these details were not later additions). For example, in the dream the shooting took place in a hotel lobby (or something similar) off which there was a roomful

TOP: *Jeane Dixon, probably the most famous of modern psychics. She is recorded as having had a precognitive vision of the assassination of John F Kennedy. While the vision she had was interesting, and possibly indeed precognitive, later writers have tended to 'gild the lily' when describing it.* **RIGHT:** *The Titanic being towed out of Southampton Docks preparatory to her fatal departure in 1912. Stories concerning passengers who cancelled at the last moment because of precognitive dreams are legion. It is difficult now to evaluate these accounts, but certainly there were many last-minute cancellations.*

of young people, and this proved indeed to be the case. However, according to the dream Kennedy was shot by a single bullet fired by an assassin hidden behind a grating in the ceiling, whereas in reality Sirhan Sirhan was in the lobby in front of Kennedy. Oddly, though, the coroner's report indicated that Kennedy died from a single bullet fired only a few inches from the back of his head. Could it be, asks Vaughan, that his dream was actually a more accurate version of events than the police reports and the video tapes? If Vaughan is ever shown to have been correct, then the case for paranormal dreaming will have been proved.

Most disasters attract claims of precognitive dreaming. To judge by the tales told after the sinking of the *Titanic*, it is surprising that there were any passengers on board. None of the claims can now be sensibly evaluated (although,

interestingly, one of the claimed precognitive dreamers was the novelist Graham Greene, then aged five). The same sort of thing happened before the 1966 Aberfan disaster, when an avalanche of slurry in Wales killed 144 people, mainly children. The psychologist J C Barker and the journalist Peter Fairley put out an appeal asking for examples of precognitive dreams. Of the 76 reports received an astonishingly high number, 22 (29 per cent), were backed up by supporting statements from people who had been told of the dream by the dreamer *before the actual event took place*. Barker and Fairley were inspired to set up an organization called the Premonitions Bureau, with the aim of collecting accounts of such precognition in order to obviate or at least ameliorate further disasters. The results were inconclusive, and the experiment ended within a few years.

A rather more scientific study along similar lines had been set up in 1947 by the British psychiatrist, Alice Buck. She and her colleagues kept detailed dream diaries and then compared their records to see if 'partial predictions' could be pieced together, jigsaw-fashion, to produce something more definite. Their most impressive series of results came in 1954-55, when they made what seemed to be quite startlingly accurate predictions of the various Comet aircraft disasters. The most fascinating part of this series of dreams is that, with hindsight, a lot of the dream-images seem to point at metal fatigue in the Comet aircraft; only later was it discovered that the disasters did indeed spring from the fact that the Comet was, by the nature of its design, prone to vibration-induced metal fatigue, the direct cause of the accidents.

Dream-premonitions of deaths can take strange forms. In the early 1980s a Devon widow named Audrey Atkinson dreamed of a death and a funeral cortège, and over the next few weeks quietly assumed that 'her number was up'. When in due course the circumstances of the funeral were 'replayed' in real life it proved that the person who had died was a man whom she had not known but who had lived a few doors away from her.

Looking through the files of paranormal dreams, it is immediately obvious that they score their most resounding successes when dealing with trivia. An astonishing example concerns a 1942 dream of Laura Dale, of the American Society for Psychical Research. Her dream involved a dog and an exploding vacuum-cleaner, and she told other people about it simply because it was so outrageous. However, a few days later she was at the movies and saw a cartoon involving, believe it or not, a dog and an exploding vacuum-cleaner. If this was precognition at work, and it certainly seems like it, one can only ask: why?

Trivial seeming too, were the precognitive dreams of John Godley, later Lord Kilbracken. In 1946 he began to dream about being at horse-races, and soon he noticed parallels between the races of his dreams and those which in fact later took place. By use of a little detective work (typically, the names of the horses in his dreams did not exactly match up with those of their real-life counterparts), he found that he could earn himself a highly useful ancillary income. Over the years Lord Kilbracken's 'powers' waned somewhat, but he nevertheless became a very successful newspaper tipster and there have been a number of other cases like Godley's.

Prediction through dreams – oneiromancy – certainly seems to occur, not very often, not very reliably, and rarely unambiguously. How can we explain this?

The most famous attempt to do this has been that of J W Dunne, who in An Experiment with Time and later books put forward his idea of 'serial time'. This is a complicated notion, but in essence he said that, for prediction to be possible, the future must in some sense 'already have happened'. He therefore posited two different 'sorts' of time: 'Time 1', which is our everyday sort of time, and 'Time 2', relative to which the 'flow' of 'Time 1' is measured – rather as you might measure the speed of a river current relative to the river's banks.

He suggested that the dreaming mind naturally operates in 'Time 2', from which vantage-point it can see the whole of 'Time 1', both future and past. The idea has its philosophical attractions, but it suffers from a grave disadvantage. If indeed there is a 'Time 2', then what is it measured against? Presumably 'Time 3', itself measured against 'Time 4' . . . and so ad infinitum.

A fashionable explanation of precognitive dreams is that they are spawned from our right-brains, which are capable of performing all sorts of acts that our left-brains consider impossible – i.e., paranormal. Although interesting, this theory is not very helpful, in that we are still left with no clue as to how precognition could possibly work under these circumstances.

A more reasonable suggestion (although superficially a much less likely one) is that it is not so much that our right-brains predict the future as that they mould it. If indeed the right-brain is responsible for poltergeist activity (see page 44), then there seems little reason why it cannot make a few small changes to present reality which have vast consequences days or years in the future. In other words, it may well be that our dreams are not so much warning us of future events as informing us of the end-results of the set of circumstances which our right-brain has just set in train.

A rather different possibility concerns patterns. We are all familiar with hunches – the 'everyday paranormal experience'. A reasonable explanation of these is that the right-brain has drawn together elements and trends unobserved by our conscious left-brain, and has extrapolated from these the inevitable – or, at least, probable – outcome. Perhaps the same process is responsible for the fact that through dreams we seem to be given, on occasion, a rather more definitive statement of likely future events.

CLAIRVOYANCE

CLAIRVOYANCE AND TELEPATHY would seem to be inextricably linked and it is an area where there has been much investigation.

These kinds of experiences, which relate to the sub-conscious, often manifest themselves in dreams.

In the late 19th century Miss R H Busk had a curious dream:

I dreamt that I was walking in a wood in my father's place in Kent, in a spot well known to me, where there was sand under the firs; I stumbled over some objects, which proved to be the heads, left protruding, of some ducks buried in the sand. The idea impressed me as so comical that I fortunately mentioned it at breakfast next morning. . .

For students of clairvoyance this was indeed a fortunate occurrence, for Miss Busk went on to relate that

only an hour later it happened that the old bailiff of the place came up for some instructions unexpectedly, and as he was leaving he said he must tell us a strange thing that had happened: there had been a robbery in the farmyard, and some stolen ducks had been found buried in the sand, with their heads protruding, in the very spot where I had seen the same.

This dream is possibly the best evidence that there is indeed such a phenomenon as clairvoyance – the ability to perceive things 'at a distance'. It is a little-known fact that foxes, when stealing poultry, will on occasion bury the unfortunate birds up to their necks, one at a time, going back for the next victim. Clearly this fact was quite unknown to Miss Busk; from her account, it seems to have been unknown to the bailiff as well. It is hard to think of a simpler explanation than that, in her dream, Miss Busk was experiencing clairvoyance.

It is difficult to draw the line between clairvoyance, precognition, telepathy and OOBEs (out-of-body experiences). Miss Busk's experience could be interpreted in several ways. Perhaps she 'saw in advance' the tale the bailiff would tell her; perhaps she had telepathic contact, as she slept in the early hours of the morning, with the people discovering the ducks; perhaps she had an OOBE, whereby she actually visited the site. As with so much of the paranormal, definitive explanations are not easy. All we can say is that, unless

Miss Busk was lying through her teeth, she had a paranormal experience of some kind – and 'clairvoyance' is as good a tag as any to apply to it.

As with precognition, we find that the vast majority of clairvoyant experiences concern matters of the utmost triviality. There are no records of clairvoyants perceiving, shall we say, the build-up to the Russian invasion of Afghanistan, yet there are lots of records of curiosities such as Miss Busk's apparently clairvoyant dream about the ducks.

The Seven Spinal Chakras, by M K Scralian. In 1971 this picture was projected in front of the audience at a Grateful Dead concert, and all present were asked to concentrate on it. The aim was to see if the psychic Malcolm Bessent would be able to 'pick up' the picture in his dreams. In fact, he gave a reasonable description. However, an even better description was given from her dreams by Felicia Parise, a young psychic who had been operating as a 'control' for Bessent.

Research into clairvoyance has been going on apace in the United States during the 1980s. Some of this has been academic (does it really happen?), while some of it has been commercial (at least one company will give you psychic advice as to what to do with your stocks and shares). Pioneers in the field were Montague Ullman and Stanley Krippner at the Maimonides Medical Center. In 1971 they asked the rock group, The Grateful Dead, to cooperate in an experiment. The band was giving a series of six concerts 50 miles or more from where the British clairvoyant Malcolm Bessent would be sleeping. Each night the audience were asked to concentrate for a short while on a picture projected behind the band, and to try to 'send' it to Bessent. The night they showed a painting by M K Scralian called *The Seven Spinal Chakras* Bessent's description was very close indeed. However, unknown to anyone except the experimenters, there was a control being run: Felicia Parise, who was show-ing signs of being an interesting clairvoyant, likewise recorded her dreams for the Maimonides team. Two days after *The Seven Spinal Chakras* had been projected, but long before the results had been correlated and the information passed back, she came out with a description of the painting that is quite chilling in its accuracy.

Another startling example of clairvoyance came in an experiment conducted by Harold Puthoff and Russell Targ at the Stanford Research Institute. Here the 'guinea pig' was Ingo Swann, who has since become an internationally renowned psychic. Swann was given an accurate statement of the latitude and longitude of a site and told to describe what he saw there. He said that he could see a mountainous island, and was promptly told that he was wrong: the latitude and longitude indicated a part of the Indian Ocean where there were no islands. It was only later that the experimenters discovered that there was indeed an island in exactly that situation, and that at its eastern end rose mountains.

It is worth noting an example of apparent clairvoyance that concerned something other than trivia. In World War II John Barnett was stationed in Nigeria, and at the height of the U-boat campaign his wife, Muriel, went out to join him. One night he was startled out of his sleep, sat bolt upright in bed, and watched the play of bright, flickering lights all over his bedroom walls. Some days later, when his wife arrived, he described the experience to her. It turned out that, while he was having this 'vision', she was undergoing the convoy's sole U-boat alert, standing in her life-saver on deck in the middle of the night, watching the searchlights of the destroyers flickering on the water.

Clairvoyance, telepathy or coincidence? It is very hard to say. Coincidence is a possibility, but the synchronism is not easy to explain, and neither is the precise nature of the 'vis-ion'. Really, we are left with a choice between telepathy and clairvoyance; and the evidence is such that clairvoyance seems the better option.

Scrying is the use of an object – such as a bowl of water or a crystal ball – as a way of focusing your attention in order to assist clairvoyance. It has to be said right at the outset that scrying has for centuries been the refuge of knaves and rogues intent on impressing their gullible fellows very often for personal gain.

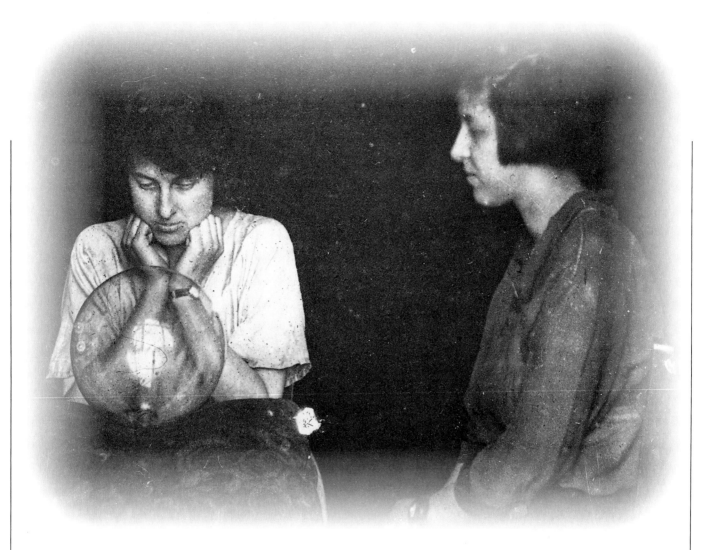

The classic case is that of Edward Kelley, the long-time companion of the great 16th-century mystic and polymath, John Dee.

Kelley claimed to have been given a magic crystal by what he called 'angels', from whom he could now receive messages through staring at the crystal. Dee spent a number of years noting down Kelley's dictation, which was, on the face of it, gibberish. However, Dee was able to 'decode' the language used, which he called 'Enochian'. Strangely, this language has a consistent syntax and grammar.

It may be that Dee's subconscious was responsible for all the notes, or it may be that Kelley was an extremely clever

*Russell Targ **FAR LEFT** and Harold Puthoff **LEFT** whose work together has done much to bring a new respectability to studies of clairvoyance and other forms of ESP.*
ABOVE: *The traditional image of the clairvoyant staring into the crystal ball. The use of an object – whether it be a crystal ball, a pool of water, or whatever – in clairvoyance is technically termed scrying, and has been practised for untold centuries. The popular notion that it is the object that 'does the magic' is of course erroneous. The most likely explanation is that it acts merely as a focus for the clairvoyant's right-brain.*

trickster; Dee came to the latter conclusion when Kelley's 'angels' announced that he, Kelley, should sleep with Dee's wife!

Assuming that people are capable of clairvoyance, then it is fair to say that the ability is obviously closely related to that of precognition. In fact, it is tempting to suggest that clairvoyance actually *is* precognition. For example, J W Dunne, in his famous 'experiment with time', had a dream which, he was convinced, told him of the occurrence of the Mont Pelée disaster of 1902. In his dream he was 'told' that 4,000 people had been killed. Much later the news of the disaster reached South Africa, where Dunne then lived. The subsidiary headline of the newspaper report he read ran, PROBABLE LOSS OF OVER 40,000 LIVES, and he read '40,000' as '4,000'. It was only about 15 years later that he noticed his misreading.

So was Dunne experiencing clairvoyance or precognition? The evidence suggests the latter, because in fact the newspaper report was quite wrong about the number of casualties. It is much more likely that Dunne foresaw himself reading the newspaper account than that he had a direct clairvoyant dream of the disaster as it happened.

From this incident, and a host of others in the literature, we get the impression that clairvoyance is not what it seems: rather than being 'far-seeing' it is the precognitive ability to foresee information that one will later receive. Of course, there is something of a time-loop at work here: Dunne would not have been so impressed by the newspaper story had it not been for his dream, and his dream would not have etched itself so firmly into his consciousness had it not been for its later apparent vindication by the newspaper report of the actuality.

What then of scrying? Whether it helps the individual to be precognitive or clairvoyant, how does it function? The probability is that the object gazed at – be it a crystal ball, tealeaves or whatever – acts much in the same way as the swinging watch of the hypnotist: it allows the left-brain to 'switch off' so that the right-brain can take over. In other words, the scryer is engaging in an exercise of self-hypnosis, yet the left-brain is remaining alert enough to record the images transmitted by the right-brain. That this might be the case is certainly evident to anyone who has been hypnotized. The experience is most curious: although your left-brain is conscious throughout all of what is going on, it 'takes a holiday', as it were, and allows the words of the hypnotist to enter the right-brain directly, without any prior intellectual analysis.

There are other reasons to believe that scrying is a form of self-hypnosis. Experiments done over the past decade or two have used hypnosis to allow people to recall their (apparent) previous incarnations, while people in the dream-state – which is, in certain ways, like the hypnotic trance – have, like Dunne, been capable of some form or another of extrasensory perception (ESP). It is rather alarming to think that people 'reading' tealeaves or looking at Tarot cards are actually – unless they are charlatans – hypnotizing themselves, yet this seems the most likely explanation.

RIGHT: A volunteer submits to a Ganzfeld (GZ) experiment. The conditions represent a half-way stage between normality and total sensory deprivation; white noise is played through the headphones, and the soothing red light is filtered and diffused through halved table-tennis balls fixed in front of the subject's eyes. In a distant room a person acting as 'transmitter' concentrates on a picture. The completely relaxed volunteer speaks in steam-of-consciousness fashion about the mental images that appear. A number of comparative tests have been done between groups of volunteers in the GZ state and control groups, and the results have been startling; consistently the GZ volunteers have scored substantially higher in apparently 'picking up' details of the 'transmitted' pictures.

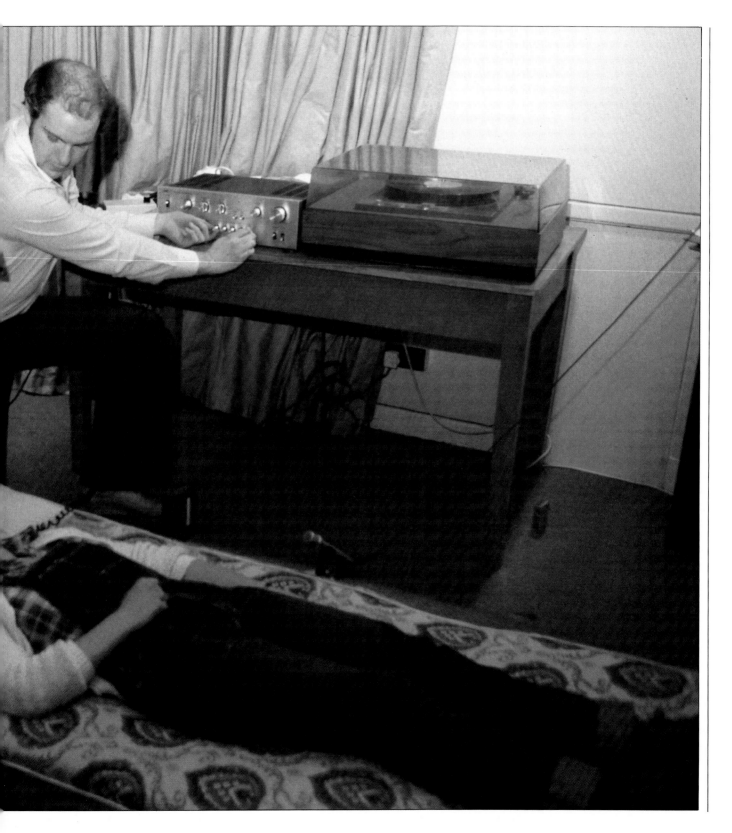

OUT-OF-BODY EXPERIENCES

 OUT-OF-BODY EXPERIENCES, universally known as OOBEs (to rhyme with 'rubies'), work two ways. First there are the experiences countless people have had of seeming to leave their body temporarily, either to visit the afterlife, as has been frequently reported in cases of people who have recovered from near-death, or simply to travel far from their physical bodies. Second there are instances of people appearing – miles away from where they actually are – in front of their friends or acquaintances. One can explain the former type of experience fairly simply in terms of orthodox psychology; the latter is a little less easy to explain.

The celebrated American psychic Jeane Dixon has told of an experience of the latter type. She lived many miles from her elderly father. One night, she reports, she woke from 'an unusually deep sleep' to find a spectre of her father by her bedside. He told her that he'd come to say farewell, and encouraged her to keep up her psychic work, because it was doing good. As you might expect, when Dixon telephoned her sister shortly afterwards, she discovered that her father had just died.

There are countless examples of dying parents coming to say a last farewell to their offspring, usually in dreams, but often enough to a person who is wide-awake – or, at least, a person who *thinks* he or she is wide-awake. The distinction is an important one. A person who is on the verge of falling asleep is capable of having so-called 'hypnagogic' dreams, and these have a strikingly high level of apparent reality. Most of us have had the experience of half falling asleep while reading. The plot of our book gets more and more curious until we finally realize what is going on and switch the light out. This is a very mild form of hypnagogic dream. People who are regular hypnagogic dreamers will tell you how vividly 'real' the visions are. (Both Robert Louis Stevenson and Edgar Allan Poe deliberately encouraged their hypnagogic dreams in order to get ideas for stories.) Analogous to hypnagogic dreams are hypnopompic ones, experienced just as you awake: Dixon's experience sounds very like a hypnopompic 'dream, a hypothesis supported by the facts that, first, she knew her father was dying, and, second, she herself mentions that she had just awoken.

Perhaps one can give a similar explanation of the curious OOBE case involving the novelists John Cowper Powys and

Theodore Dreiser. The two had dined together at Dreiser's home in New York, and as Powys departed he mysteriously told Dreiser that he would visit him later that night. Dreiser thought, quite naturally, that Powys was joking. However, a couple of hours afterwards, Dreiser suddenly saw Powys standing at the door of his room. He moved towards Powys, asking rather crossly how he had done the 'trick', but the spectre disappeared. The real-life Powys, on being telephoned, refused to make any comment on the matter.

It is tempting to say that all that happened was that Dreiser, having registered his friend's somewhat curious farewell remark, was drowsing and had a hypnagogic dream; Powys's refusal to comment could then simply be seen as a facet of his known fondness for being enigmatic. Yet to Dreiser the spectral 'visit' of Powys was something very real: he did not doubt for a moment that his friend was actually, in some form, there. It is a very great pity that there was no one with Dreiser at the time, because then we could establish whether or not this was an OOBE rather than a hypnagogic dream.

Experiences such as Dixon's and Dreiser's can be explained as hypnagogic dreaming, but there are other possibilities. One is that their 'visitors' deliberately projected themselves out of their material bodies. Another is that the 'visited' somehow drew the projections out of the 'visitors'. In neither case have we any evidence that the 'visitor' knew of the phenomenon.

The other type of OOBE is that in which the person directly involved knows that he has left his body. In 1863 S R Wilmot sailed from England to rejoin his family in the United States. He shared a cabin with one William Tait. One night Wilmot 'saw' his wife, clad only in her nightie, enter the cabin, hesitate when she saw someone else there, and then conquer her shyness to come over to his bunk and kiss him.

It is not unnatural that spouses separated for a long time should have such visions. What startled Wilmot, however, was that in the morning Tait accused him of being a rakehell: he too had seen this scantily clad woman entering the cabin and behaving with a certain lack of decorum. To make the matter even odder, on his arrival in New York Wilmot was asked by his wife whether he remembered the 'visit'; she described exactly what had happened, and on subsequent questioning was able to give details of the general layout of the cabin.

Various scientific experiments have been done on OOBEs, notably by Harold Puthoff and Russell Targ. The conclusion from all such tests has to be that OOBEs do genuinely occur. Why they should, and how, is a matter of mystery.

LEFT: One of the most astonishing accounts of an OOBE concerns the two writers Theodore Dreiser and John Cowper Powys, the latter apparently projecting his image to visit the former. In this unusual photograph we see Dreiser contemplating a bust of Powys. **ABOVE, LEFT:** *Robert Louis Stevenson and* **RIGHT:** *Edgar Allan Poe, two writers who deliberately exploited the visions which they saw in the hypnagogic state in order to create their fictions.*

TIMESLIPS

IN 1911 ELEANOR JOURDAIN and Charlotte Moberly, two Oxford dons, published the book *An Adventure*. In it they recounted a curious experience which they had shared when visiting the Palace of Versailles in 1901. Wandering through the gardens, they found themselves in 1789, just before the downfall of the French monarchy. They encountered people dressed in the clothing of that age who talked of the current (1789) political situation. Somehow the two women had slipped back in time. There are rationalist explanations. For example, there

was a fancy-dress party in Versailles in 1894, and it is possible that the two women stumbled into it. However, there is a big difference between 1894 and 1901.

Reports of such phenomena are rare, but they are convincing. Take the example of Jane O'Neill, who in 1973 suffered a severe shock (she helped free people trapped after a particularly nasty traffic accident). After this she began to have a number of paranormal experiences, the most significant of which concerned a visit to Fotheringhay Church, England. She found herself particularly fascinated by one picture, and later mentioned this fact to the friend who had been with her. To her amazement, the friend said that she had seen no such picture. Mrs O'Neill was concerned enough to make some enquiries, and eventually found that she had 'seen' the interior of the church as it had been in the 1500s. Somehow, she had 'travelled' back several hundred years.

Such accounts are reminiscent of presumed 'reincarnatory' dreams, in which people seem to recall their previous existences. An intriguing experiment in this field was carried out by a group headed by the Australian writer, G M Glaskin, during the 1970s. Typically, the experimenter would lie down, shoes off, and have his or her ankles and pineal region (the centre of the forehead) massaged by assistants; then one of the assistants would instruct the experimenter to go through a number of psychic exercises before returning to a 'past life'.

The results were astonishing: the experimenters had stunningly vivid experiences of what they believed to be earlier incarnations. One, a bisexual, was fellated superbly by a male prostitute in a Roman 'pleasure palace', yet his real-life body failed to show the signs of his experience. Others believed that, as well as reliving previous incarnations, they had travelled forward in time to experience future ones. One of Glaskin's own 'journeys' was of particular interest in that, some while later, he visited the British Museum and was able to pinpoint his vision as having occurred about 5,000 years earlier in the Faiyum, Egypt. He had had not the slightest interest in Egyptology before making this discovery, and so concludes that he genuinely experienced a few hours of life in a past age.

Is it possible to slip back into a previous era? According to our modern understanding of the physical laws that define the universe, it is very difficult indeed to 'visit' the future and equally difficult to *affect* the past. However, there is nothing in modern science that prohibits merely 'visiting' the past.

An exciting piece of evidence – and one that is so far totally lacking – might be an historical record of a stranger appearing for a short while in, say, the 17th century, sporting a Mohican cut and clad in blue jeans. It is possible that there are indeed such records, as we shall see when we look at cases of 'appearing people', but as yet we have to conclude that the evidence is indicative rather than compelling. Nevertheless, the Misses Moberly and Jourdain are unlikely candidates for hoaxers, and anyway they ran the risk of losing their professional respectability by publishing their accounts of what they seem genuinely to have believed to be a timeslip. Until we have evidence to the contrary, we have to take their accounts at face value.

ABOVE LEFT: *Le Petit Trianon at Versailles.* **RIGHT:** *Fotheringhay Church, seen over the waters of the River Nene. It was here in 1973 that Jane O'Neill experienced what seems to have been a timeslip, seeing the interior of the church as it had been several hundred years before.*

Eleanor Jourdain **LEFT** and Charlotte Moberly **ABOVE** the two respectable English gentlewomen who seemed to travel back in time by over a century during a visit to Versailles. No one has yet offered a convincing rationalist explanation for their experience.

REINCARNATION

DESPITE OCCASIONAL NEWSPAPER REPORTS to the contrary, depressingly few Western scientists are remotely interested in the paranormal: most regard it as either a load of nonsense or, at best, something totally outside their own field of investigation. Among the few who are prepared at least to give the paranormal a hearing, the subject of reincarnation (the transmigration of souls) is probably the most unpopular. Eastern scientists, by contrast, are much more at home with the idea. This is not solely for religious reasons: the oriental world-view is simply different from the occidental one.

Even so, the evidence in both East and West is discomfitingly favourable towards reincarnation, however much it might upset one's sensibilities. There are countless cases of people who seem to be able to remember past lives. Many of these people 'recall' that they were members of the royal family of Atlantis, and we can with some confidence ignore their 'recollections', since the Atlantean royal family could have been only of a certain size, after all; but others 'remember' lives that were, while not exactly humdrum, at least fairly consistent with the age. And it seems reasonable to assume that people who came to sticky ends might have less difficulty in 'remembering' their previous incarnations than the rest of us. For example, the likelihood of your having been of the French upper classes in a previous life is, in statistical terms, fairly remote – but if you travelled in the tumbril and perished under the guillotine there is a better-than-usual chance that you might 'remember' your former existence – or, at least, the end of it.

The British writer Joan Grant, author of a number of historical novels she claimed were based on her own past-life experiences, accepted this aspect of reincarnation in her

BELOW: The Temple of Poseidon, Atlantis, as rendered in Sir Gerald Hargreaves' 1954 book Atalanta. Tales of living people who had earlier lives in Atlantis are widely regarded as nonsense.

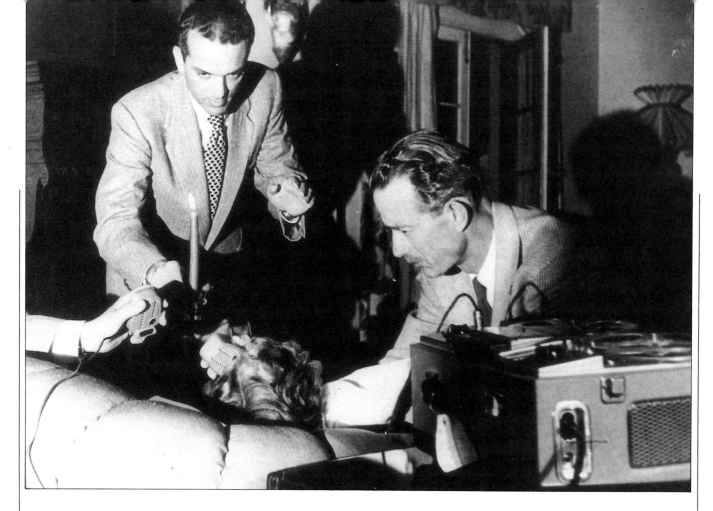

explanation of alcoholism. She suggested that alcoholics in this life had died from thirst in some previous one. Even more plausibly, she drew attention to the times when wounded combatants ended their days in crude military hospitals where the only anaesthetic was cheap rotgut alcohol: if you died, say, at Waterloo, eagerly wondering when your next swig of poteen would come, it is no wonder if in this life you drain every bottle in sight.

Theories like this one are, of course, risible – but only superficially so. It seems far more likely that a powerful emotion could survive transmigration than that detailed memories could, particularly since most of those 'detailed memories' prove on examination to be dubious. One of the most famous recent cases is that of a Colorado woman who, under hypnotic regression, told tales of her earlier life as 'Bridey Murphy', an Irish girl who lived in the early 19th century. The details she recounted of the Ireland of that time were very convincing; yet the whole set of evidence is devalued because, as a child, she had an old Irish nanny. It seems most likely that the tales told as bedtime stories 'implanted' themselves in the child's mind, later emerging under hypnosis.

The same scepticism has to be exercised when thinking of Joan Grant's 'recollections': she seems to have had an astonishingly distinguished set of incarnations, being, *inter alia*, a French princess at the time of the Revolution and that rarest of all things, a female Egyptian pharaoh – one of whose adventures was a trip to Atlantis!

Another novelist who could 'recall' being an Atlantean was Taylor Caldwell. At the age of 12 she produced a book called *The Romance of Atlantis*, purportedly based on her dream-memories of her life as the empress of Atlantis around the time of that continent's demise. The book was not published until 1975 (revised by Jess Stearn). However much one might wish to claim that this was because its contents were a shock to the intellect, the truth is that it contains sufficient inconsistencies and outright howlers to render it poor evidence. In light of the fact that the book was written by a 12-year-old, it seems significant that the name of the Atlantean princess was 'Salustra' and that the man she loved was the Emperor of 'Althrustri'.

ABOVE: *'Ruth Simmons', in reality Virginia Tighe, undergoing regression hypnosis with Morey Bernstein* **ON LEFT:** *In these conditions she seemed to recall an earlier lifetime as a 19th-century Irishwoman, Bridey Murphy. Bernstein's experiments are often cited as proof of the phenomenon of reincarnation, yet there are other possible explanations.* **RIGHT:** *Some years after the 'Bridey Murphy' sessions, Tighe and Bernstein examine a selection of the voluminous mail he received on the subject in the wake of his bestselling and controversial book,* The Search for Bridey Murphy *(1956).*
TOP RIGHT: *The case of Lurancy Vennum has been widely reported as a good example of reincarnation. In 1877, under hypnosis, she indicated that, in some way, her body contained an additional personality, that of a girl who had died a year or so earlier. The parents of the dead child were convinced, and Lurancy lived with them for a few months until the 'extra' personality departed.*

However, some of the evidence discovered in India during this century has strongly supported reincarnation. Take the case of Sai Baba of Puttaparti, born there in 1926. He claims to be the reincarnation of the great Indian mystic, Sai Baba of Shirdi, who died in 1918. Until the age of 14 he was like any other child, but then he was struck down by a mysterious illness that rendered him delirious for a long period. During this time he would burst into long passages of Vedantic philosophy, speak in tongues, sing songs, recite poetry and so forth. It would be all too easy to dismiss Baba's claims of a previous life were it not for the fact that he seems to be capable of performing miracles.

The classic text on reincarnation is Ian Stevenson's *Twenty Cases Suggestive of Reincarnation* (1966). In his later book, *Cases of the Reincarnation Type*, Stevenson recounted the tale of a child called Jasbir Lal Jat, who died of smallpox at the age of three. Before he was buried, however, Jasbir 'came to life', as it were. A few weeks later he was capable of normal conversation, and now the child claimed to be the son of a Brahmin who lived in Vehedi. Rather unpleasantly, he refused to eat the meals cooked by his mother because he was of higher caste than his parents. Some years later, his village was visited by a Brahmin whom Jasbir immediately claimed to be his aunt. She was initially sceptical, but Jasbir's behaviour on travelling to Vehedi was enough to convince her and others that he truly was a reincarnation of Sobha Ram, a youth who had died of smallpox around the time that Jasbir had himself 'died'.

Evidence from the West is more scanty, but some of it is uncomfortably convincing. One case is that of Lurancy Vennum of Watseka, Illinois, who in 1877, at the age of 13, told her doctor under hypnosis that she was under the protection of an 'angel' called Mary Roff. It proved that there had indeed been a Mary Roff living in the same town; she had died about a year after Lurancy's birth. Mary's parents were confident enough that their daughter's spirit 'lived on' in Lurancy to allow the child to move in with them for three months or so. At the end of this period Lurancy became Lurancy once more, and she rejoined her own family.

It is all very well to cite cases of apparent reincarnation, but this does not help us to answer two significant questions. First, *how* does it happen? Second, *why* does it happen? The Buddhist response to both questions is simply that reincarnation is one part of the cycle of human life: it happens because it happens, and that is the way the universe works. Another possibility quoted is that there are, as it were, only so many souls to go around; consequently they have to be 'recycled'. Neither of these explanations is particularly pleasing. A third possibility is that we, on earth, are merely small parts of the lives of cosmic beings, who choose to 'reside' for a while in human form; bearing in mind the misery of the average human life, this seems implausible (not to mention all the other reasons why it seems implausible!).

There is no viable rationale for reincarnation, and no perceivable mechanism, and so there is little reason to believe that it actually occurs — except that the evidence in its favour is so strong and refuses to go away.

PSYCHOKINESIS

ONE DAY, A BOY Uri Geller, received an electric shock from his mother's sewing-machine. The rest, as they say, is history – or possibly so. It is infernally hard to determine whether Geller is a complete sham, a person genuinely able to mould objects through mental effort alone, or a mixture of the two. Certainly most of his metal-bending effects can be achieved by a competent conjurer, as James 'The Amazing' Randi has demonstrated all over the world. Equally certainly, a good number of paranormally able people have traced the emergence of their powers to some kind of sudden physical or emotional trauma.

Psychokinesis – often called 'telekinesis' – is the ability to move objects through the use of the mind, and it obeys the general rule we have noticed about the paranormal: the more offensive to common sense a particular phenomenon is, the better is the evidence for it. Geller's spoon-bending is a case in point. In fact, it takes only a little skill to make people – even television cameras – believe that you are bending a rod of metal simply by stroking it; but a spoon is a different matter. Professional conjurers such as James Randi have little trouble in doing the trick, but this hardly explains how, after a 1973 television appearance by Geller, children all over Great Britain apparently became able paranormally to wreck the contents of their parents' cutlery drawer.

John Taylor, Professor of Mathematics at King's College, London, performed some fairly rigorous experiments on a number of such children, and became convinced that indeed they were not cheating. Later he was to 'recant', saying that the paranormal was all bunk; yet he was never satisfactorily to explain why it was that children appeared to be able to bend cutlery sealed, for example, in airtight glass containers.

The classic object to move is one's own body, and indeed there are widespread reports of levitation by various gurus and their acolytes. It is hard to know how to evaluate these. One fan of transcendental meditation who went on a course which claimed to teach people to levitate was later heard having the following conversation with a friend:

Friend: And did you actually *fly?*
Fan: Well . . . almost.

However, levitation cannot be dismissed out of hand. The 19th-century British medium, Daniel Dunglas Home, frequently flew, unless we are to discount the evidence of numerous perfectly sober and respectable witnesses. Sai Baba has done the same in India during this century (again subject to the same *caveat*).

Some people believe themselves to be gifted gamblers, in that they reckon they can predict the way the dice or the cards

OPPOSITE: *Sai Baba, to whom psychokinesis seems merely a matter of child's play*
LEFT: *The Swiss metal-bender Silvio Meyer* ON LEFT *undergoing some scientific testing.* TOP: *Professor John Taylor examines some deformed cutlery.*

ABOVE: It is hard to deny the evidence presented by a photograph such as this one – which seems almost certainly not to be a fake. W E Cox claims to have an 'entity' friend, who is here writing a message to him. Current models of psychokinesis would suggest that the 'entity' is in fact Cox's right-brain – but, of course, these are all just theories. **ABOVE CENTRE:** A message from Cox's 'entity' friend. **ABOVE RIGHT:** Three frames from a cine film of the same series of experiments. showing an aluminium bar emerging through the front glass of the mini-lab.

UPPER LEFT: Researcher W E Cox demonstrates an inflated balloon in a sealed box. This might seem rather uninteresting until one learns that the balloon was not inflated when it was placed in the box. And, just to make sure, the neck of the balloon had been sealed using superglue. **LEFT:** In an extended series of experiments on psychokinesis carried out in Missouri there were some astonishing results – including this example of a table being levitated.

LEFT: *The apparent levitation of a table in one of the SORRAT psychokinesis experiments carried out in Missouri. This photograph was taken on 31st October 1986.* **LOWER LEFT:** *Another SORRAT experiment saw W E Cox place solid leather rings in a sealed plastic envelope. On 26th June these rings were found to have linked; however, soon afterwards they unlinked. Many researchers are less than impressed with such 'evidence'.*

ABOVE: *SORRAT researchers Ray Christ and Joe Mangini under a 80lb (36kg) dining table seemingly levitated to the ceiling before crashing to the floor. This SORRAT experiment took place in June 1966.* **LEFT:** *The levitation of a doll during the SORRAT experiments.*

will fall. However, when J B Rhine was investigating this subject he discovered that, astonishingly, better results were obtained from people who claimed to be able to *control* the fall of the cards or dice, not merely predict them. Of course, Rhine's experimental techniques were not so rigorous as they could have been; still, one is left with the impression that his evidence for psychokinesis is a lot better than his evidence for, say, precognition. Subsequent experimenters have had similar results.

It would seem that psychokinesis, if indeed it is a genuine phenomenon, is merely a sort of subdivision of poltergeist activity, the topic at which we shall be looking next. Yes, there are people who display the most remarkable psychokinetic powers – Nina Kulagina of the Soviet Union springs to mind – but none of them can compare with the psychokinetic abilities of the average 13-year-old, assuming that he or (more usually) she is placed in a situation that is emotionally stressful.

Psychokinesis is little understood and, like so many paranormal phenomena, is likely to remain so for the foreseeable future: the ability seems to 'melt away' when subjected to rigorous scientific examination. Nevertheless, the ability of certain people mentally to manipulate their environments, even to the extent of making themselves 'fly', has been recorded so often that it is hard to consign all of the evidence to the dustbin.

A related phenomenon is psychic surgery.

Television cameras have recorded a number of instances, notably in South America, of self-styled 'surgeons' performing complex operations on people with no anaesthetics and with no more sophisticated apparatus than a penknife – sometimes without knives at all, simply pulling the tissues apart. The patients have remained conscious throughout the proceedings, and on some occasions have shown an active interest in their own

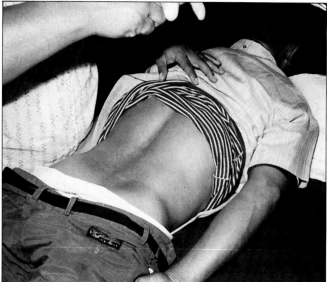

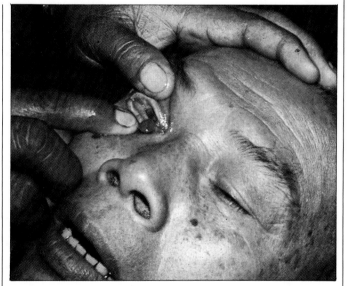

OPPOSITE: *The researcher J G Pratt conducting an experiment on psychokinesis using a dice-tumbling machine. Since the subject was not in physical contact with the dice, there was no apparent way in which she could influence the way in which they fell. Tests like this one have produced much better scientific evidence in favour of psychokinesis than has ever been adduced in the case of, say, telepathy, yet people are more prepared to believe in telepathy than in psychokinesis.* **THIS PAGE:** *Photographs of psychic surgery in action are usually the stuff of nightmares rather than of dreams! That psychic surgery is practised is an undisputed fact, yet modern science has no explanation whatsoever to explain why this can be so. Many paranormal researchers regard it as a manifestation of the psychokinetic ability.*

revealed intestines (one reason for doubting the camera records; most people exposed to their own innards pass out rather than look intrigued). Assuming psychic surgery is not some grand hoax, and there is little reason to believe that it is so, then some kind of psychokinetic phenomenon must be at work.

The rational, occidental left-brain consciousness has a great deal of difficulty in taking psychokinesis on board. Yet the acknowledgement of psychokinesis makes many other aspects of the paranormal so much easier to understand. Of nothing is this more true than the 'poltergeist effect'.

RIGHT: The classic print of the 19th-century British medium Daniel Dunglas Home levitating in front of witnesses – the party trick to end all party tricks. No one has yet been able to produce any rationalist explanation for Home's feats, and it is impossible to believe that the witnesses were all simply lying: that would have been a conspiracy on too grand a scale. Thanks to Home, tales of levitation became all the rage in the 1860s. This 1863 Punch cartoon ABOVE: satirizes the effect of such tales on high society. FAR LEFT: A sketch of levitation from Glanvill's Saducismus Triumphatus, 1681. The 'evidence' of such drawings is not held in high regard by researchers into the paranormal. LEFT: Daniel Dunglas Home.

POLTERGEISTS

TOWARDS THE END OF 1965 a house in the state of São Paulo, Brazil, became infested by a poltergeist. A near neighbour, João Volpe, who had studied the psychic, took an interest, and soon determined that the 'focus' of the poltergeist was an 11-year-old child called Maria José Ferreira, who slept in the servants' quarters. Volpe believed the girl to be a natural spirit medium and, in fact, the cause of all the poltergeist activity – although quite without any deliberate intent. He took Maria into his own home for study, a decision his family may have resented, because soon stones were appearing from nowhere to fly around the rooms. This was no joke, since not all of the stones were pebbles: Volpe weighed one at 8lb (4.7kg). Eggs, vegetables and other items filled the air. Maria herself derived some slight benefit from all this frenzied activity; she was able to ask for goodies from the 'spirits' and immediately they would appear at her feet.

So far the 'spirits', although a considerable nuisance, displayed no malice, but then things changed radically. Maria's face and bottom were repeatedly slapped, and needles would abruptly appear implanted in her foot, even when she was fully shod: one time, 55 of these needles had to be extracted. Worse happened: Maria was at school when her clothes suddenly burst into flames, and on the same day the Volpes' bedroom did likewise.

Volpe took her to a well-respected spirit medium, and a 'spirit' came through from the 'other side' to claim responsibility for all this terror, saying that the child had been a witch in a former lifetime, and that now the spirits of those who had suffered or died because of her activities were exacting their revenge. Volpe used spiritualist techniques to ameliorate the worst horrors of the poltergeist, but nevertheless vegetables were still likely to fly through the air when Maria was around. At the age of 13 she committed suicide.

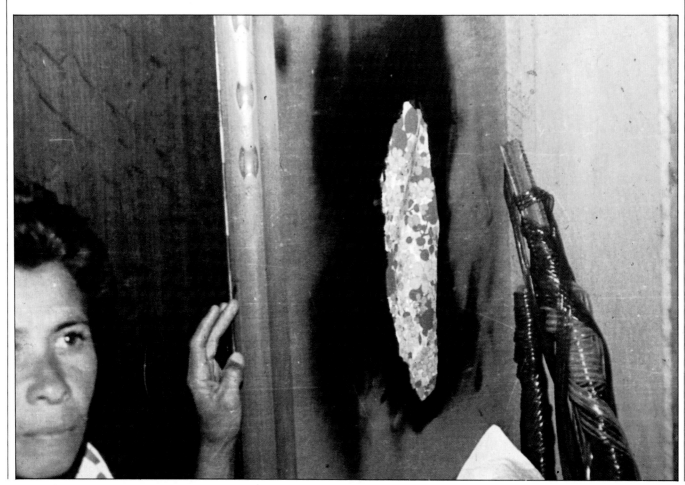

The case of Maria José Ferreira is of interest on several counts. First, it is reported by Guy Lyon Playfair (in his *The Indefinite Boundary*); it is not necessary to agree with Playfair's theories in order to respect him as a meticulous researcher. It is, of course, possible that the wool was pulled over his eyes, but it seems unlikely – although one has to add that he had no direct experience of this case. (He later did directly experience the activities of the poltergeist active in Enfield, England, between 1977 and 1979.) A second point of interest is that the poltergeist became actively malicious, which is by no means always the case with poltergeists. Indeed, poltergeist activity is usually characterized by the fact that, though it is a terrible nuisance, no one is physically harmed. When there is violence in a poltergeist case, it is usually described as one of 'demonic possession.'

The word 'poltergeist' means, literally, 'rattling ghost', and from pre-Christian times until our own it has indeed been assumed that a poltergeist is exactly that, a disembodied spirit which, for reasons hard to understand, wishes to communicate with mortals by making noises or throwing things around. The borderline between poltergeist activity and 'demonic possession' is a hazy one. The latter term is born from two assumptions: first, that poltergeist activities are indeed the product of capricious or malevolent spirits; and second that people would not wish themselves any physical harm. The second assumption is hard to justify: if some people can consciously be masochists there is no reason why other people cannot be unconsciously so. The first is more controversial. The evidence in favour of ghosts is not especially good. That there might be not only ghosts, but ghosts capable of throwing items of household furniture around, seems extremely improbable.

LEFT: *A typical example of the type of damage which poltergeists are capable of inflicting on their surroundings. This particular photograph was taken in Suzano, Brazil, in 1970. Two examples of poltergeist activity in Britain. In South Bromley* **ABOVE:** *around 1973, a poltergeist saw fit to pierce an investigator's scarf with a pin – perhaps a warning that next time it could be the investigator rather than the scarf? In fact, while poltergeists may terrorize human beings, it is very rare that they cause them any physical harm.* **TOP:** *One of the evidences from the famous case of the Enfield poltergeist, investigated during 1977-9 by Guy Lion Playfair and others. Despite the fact that they had been left in a closed drawer, these notes were singed by the poltergeist.* **TOP RIGHT:** *Evidence of fiery poltergeist activity in a 1970s São Paulo case.*

It is generally accepted that poltergeists are *the* classic paranormal phenomenon: explain poltergeist activity and so much else of the paranormal becomes explicable. One of the notable things about cases of poltergeist activity is that there is always a 'focus', typically a pubertal child (almost always a girl). Puberty is a time when the human individual experiences considerable physical and mental changes; few of us ever forget the traumas of our own puberty. It therefore seems reasonable to suggest that poltergeist activity is some sort of product of the disturbed right-brain, which is, as it were, manifesting the fact that it disagrees fundamentally with the left-brain. This idea conforms with the evidence that the usual focus of a poltergeist is a prepubertal girl, whose body's hormonal balance is in a state of flux, preparing for the onset of menstruation.

One of the most famous cases of poltergeist activity is that of the Cock Lane 'ghost' of 1759. It was investigated by a dazzling selection of 'famous names' – Samuel Johnson, David Garrick and Horace Walpole, to name but a few. The situation was complicated. Richard Parsons had taken in as lodgers at his home in Cock Lane, London, William Kent and Fanny Lynes, assuming that they were man and wife. In fact, Kent was the widower of Fanny's sister, Elizabeth, who had died in childbirth; the law stopped Fanny from marrying

him, but the two were in love, and so their only option was to 'live in sin'. Not long after the couple had moved in, Parsons borrowed 12 guineas from Kent – a useful loan, since Parsons had not only a family but a drink problem to finance. The repayments of this loan were not properly kept up. Fanny was pregnant. Finally, when Kent was away from home, Fanny requested that the Parsons' older daughter, Elizabeth, sleep with her as company during the long and scary nights.

After Elizabeth had slept several nights with Fanny, Fanny began to complain that their sleep was being disturbed by loud noises. At first it was assumed that this was merely the shoemaker in the house next door working late, but this explanation soon fell by the wayside. Although no one could come up with a reason, the house had clearly become infested by a 'rattling ghost', especially at nights, when the home was filled with the sound of inexplicable knockings.

Shortly afterwards, the pregnant Fanny believed she was in labour, and a doctor was called in. In fact, it proved that she was suffering from smallpox, and she died soon after. Two years later, in 1761, having moved away, Kent married again. However, the knockings still continued at the Parsons' home, despite clergy being called in to exorcise the 'spirit'. The various people involved in the investigation

LEFT: *A cartoon from 1762 lampoons the social luminaries who investigated the Cock Lane Ghost. A surprising number of 'household names' interested themselves in this case: William Hogarth, Horace Walpole, David Garrick, Samuel Foote, Charles Churchill, John Wesley and, last but far from least, a certain Dr Johnson.* **ABOVE:** *During late 1977 a seemingly normal home in Enfield, England, was tormented by a poltergeist. The Harper children – Rose, Janet, Pete and Jimmy – seemed to tolerate the invasion of both the 'rattling ghost' and the psychic researchers with considerable equanimity.*

soon learned how to 'communicate with the ghost' by a system of knocking. The 'ghost' claimed to be Fanny's spirit, and said that she had been poisoned by William Kent and sought justice. This was obviously highly embarrassing for Kent, who attended at least one séance to hear the verdict of his dead lover. The case began to attract considerable popular attention, and finally Kent had had enough. He took the principals to court: Parsons was sentenced to two years in prison, his wife to one, and various other people involved to shorter terms.

The reason for the prison sentences was that it was believed by the court that the knockings had been deliberately caused by young Elizabeth Parsons, and certainly this could have been the case; much later, in the 1840s, the sisters Margaret, Leah and Kate Fox perpetrated a similar hoax, which had as its by-product the creation of the modern Spiritualist movement. It is plausible to suggest that Elizabeth Parsons had a 'crush' on Fanny, and that after the older woman's death she blamed Kent for having destroyed her idol. If her resentment were conscious, then it is likely that the Cock Lane 'ghost' was a fraud; if, however, it were unconscious, then it is quite likely that the case was genuinely one of poltergeist activity. The latter explanation is by far the more tempting, for Elizabeth was at exactly the right age to be a poltergeist's 'focus'.

What, then, *is* a poltergeist? Playfair believes that poltergeists are, as it were, loose balls of spirit energy which delight in tormenting human beings to a greater or lesser degree Colin Wilson, who was one of the first to propose that poltergeists are, like so many other paranormal phenomena, products of the little-understood activities of the right-brain, more recently, after discussion with Playfair, changed his opinions and opted for the loose-spirit explanation. Jenny Randles, best known for her investigations of UFOs, has suggested that both poltergeists and UFOs represent some sort of psychic projection, and that the two phenomena have similar causes or are possibly merely different manifestations of the same phenomenon.

Randles is probably correct, and poltergeists, like UFOs, are probably products of the right-brain. Of course, such an explanation does not on its own help us very much, since it tells us nothing about the real mechanism of poltergeist activity – about how the right-brain is capable of producing such effects. Nevertheless, there are strong correlations between extended UFO cases and extended poltergeist cases. Usually a 'focus' can be found who is a child facing the onset of puberty, although sometimes the individual is older, but similarly enduring some kind of hormonal turmoil. In UFO cases it is tempting to say simply that mentally disturbed people will think they see curious things; but this explanation falls apart in instances where large numbers of people see the same UFO, or indeed when independent observers can, whether they like it or not, experience the influence of a poltergeist. Both types of phenomenon would seem to represent the physical reification of some impulse born of the unconscious (i.e., right-brain) of the 'focus'. The exact mechanism is a puzzle, but it could well be related to the model put forward earlier.

A final poltergeist case is worth brief mention. In 1878 Esther Cox was living in the house of her brother-in-law, Daniel Teed, in Amherst, Nova Scotia; other residents in this packed homestead included her two sisters (one of whom was married to Teed), her brother, and Teed's adult brother and two small sons. Esther, aged 18, seems clearly to have been at the age where she was fully sexually awakened, yet

TOP LEFT: *A sketch by J W Archer, taken from Charles Mackay's Memoirs of Extraordinary Popular Delusions (1852), showing the interior of the home in Cock Lane where the celebrated poltergeist performed. The knockings were frequently heard in the corner at the rear right.* **RIGHT:** *During 1952 the Glynn family of Runcorn, Britain, were pestered by a poltergeist. The police assumed that there was a human, rather than a paranormal, agency at work, and consistently set traps to catch the assumed culprit; despite their efforts, the poltergeist activities continued. Here we see John Glynn surveying the wreckage of his bedroom.* **UPPER RIGHT:** *Colin Wilson, the best-selling writer. He initially believed that poltergeists were manifestations of the right-brains of adolescents but, after discussions with Guy Lion Playfair, concluded that they were instead malicious bundles of psychic energy.*

as a 'nice' girl could do nothing to satisfy her desires, which she possibly did not even consciously recognize. Matters were not helped when her boyfriend attempted to force her to have sex at gunpoint. He fled Amherst in shame, but over the ensuing weeks and months the Teed household was tormented by poltergeist activities centred on Esther. Various objects caught fire, there were numerous cracks and bangs, and Esther suffered a good deal of physical punishment: she was stabbed by a penknife and a fork, hit over the head by a broom, and so forth. Possibly the most frightening incident occurred when a group of witnesses saw writing spontaneously appear on the wall above her bed: 'Esther, you are mine to kill'.

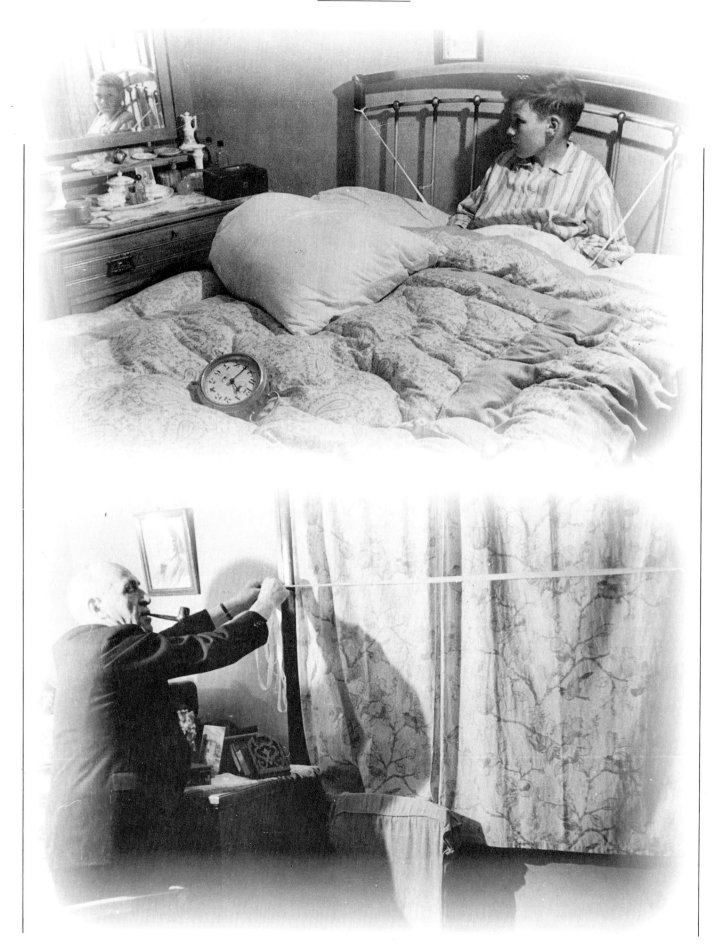

Esther herself blamed the phenomena on spirits who 'spoke to her'. Like Joan of Arc and Peter Sutcliffe, the 'Yorkshire Ripper', she heard 'voices'. In particular, the most malevolent spirit was 'Bob Nickle', a significant name, since the boy who had tried to rape her was called Bob MacNeal. However, it is clear that she was significantly mentally disturbed, and so it is highly likely that 'Bob Nickle' was

---

LEFT: *The psychic researcher Harry Price was famous in his day, but more recent studies have cast considerable doubt on the validity of his work – indeed, it seems certain that on occasion he simply cheated to create a dramatic effect. The lower picture shows him working on an alleged poltergeist case in Crawley, England, in 1945. In the upper picture we see 12-year-old Alan Rhodes, the supposed focus of the poltergeist,* **ABOVE:** *A sketch by A J Hill of the town of Amherst in 1876.*

---

purely the product of her own right-brain – creating an entity on whom all this mayhem could be blamed.

Some while later Esther was convicted of arson and imprisoned for a few months; the poltergeist activity abruptly ceased.

In an earlier age Esther might well have found herself facing a rather more fearsome sentence than a few months in prison: she could have been tortured or executed for being possessed by the devil. Numerous researchers have pointed up the similarity between cases of poltergeist activity and 'demonic possession'. Some, such as Malachi Martin, have preferred to invoke the influence of Satan, or at least a subsidiary devil. Others, such as Marc Cramer, have suggested that possession is simply a form of mental illness that has yet to be recognized by orthodox science. Both, in their way, may be correct. The torment of the right-brain can quite legitimately be described as a form of mental illness, while its malign activities could well attract the adjective 'demonic'.

AURAS

MANY PSYCHICS CLAIM to be able to see auras surrounding living beings, and to be able to tell from the colour or general circumstances of these auras whether or not the being concerned is in a good state of health.

For a long time this claim was dismissed as just so much psychic nonsense, but then in 1939 Semyon and Valentina Kirlian began a series of experiments in which they took photographs of living objects – from human hands to the leaves of trees – in a powerful electric field. They discovered that around the edges of whichever living object they photographed there was what seemed, to all intents and purposes, to be an aura. Moreover, this aura changed in colour or composition depending upon the circumstances of the person or other entity involved: someone who had just had a swig of liquor would display a brighter and more energetic aura than before.

Photographs taken in this way – nowadays universally known as 'Kirlian photographs' – have appeared in books and magazines the world over. There seems little reason to

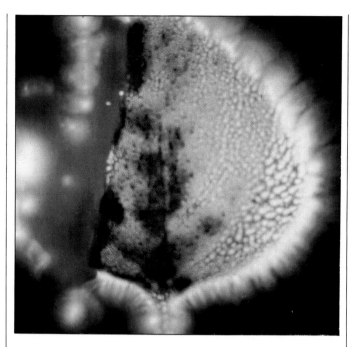

doubt that indeed living beings do possess auras. However, the nature of these is little understood; likewise, no one knows whether or not the phenomenon has any genuine significance. However, it is worth mentioning a couple of important points. Kirlian auras are not displayed by inorganic objects – such as stones – although they do persist for a while after the death of an organism. Indeed, the classic Kirlian photograph is of a leaf torn from a tree, with part of it ripped away; the aura can be seen following the contours even of the removed section. In both instances it is hard to escape the conclusion that the Kirlian aura is not just some kind of interesting electrical effect, but the genuine representation of a 'life-force' that we all possess and that extends a short distance beyond us.

*Kirlian photographs of rose leaves. One **LEFT** is healthy and whole; the other **ABOVE** has been cut. The difference in the appearance of the two auras is striking. **RIGHT**: The seeming aura around a sea fern.*

OVERLEAF: *Superb examples of abstract art? No: these are Kirlian photographs showing the auras surrounding two human fingertips. It is not difficult to see the difference between the aura of a healthy person **LEFT** and that of a drug addict **RIGHT**.*

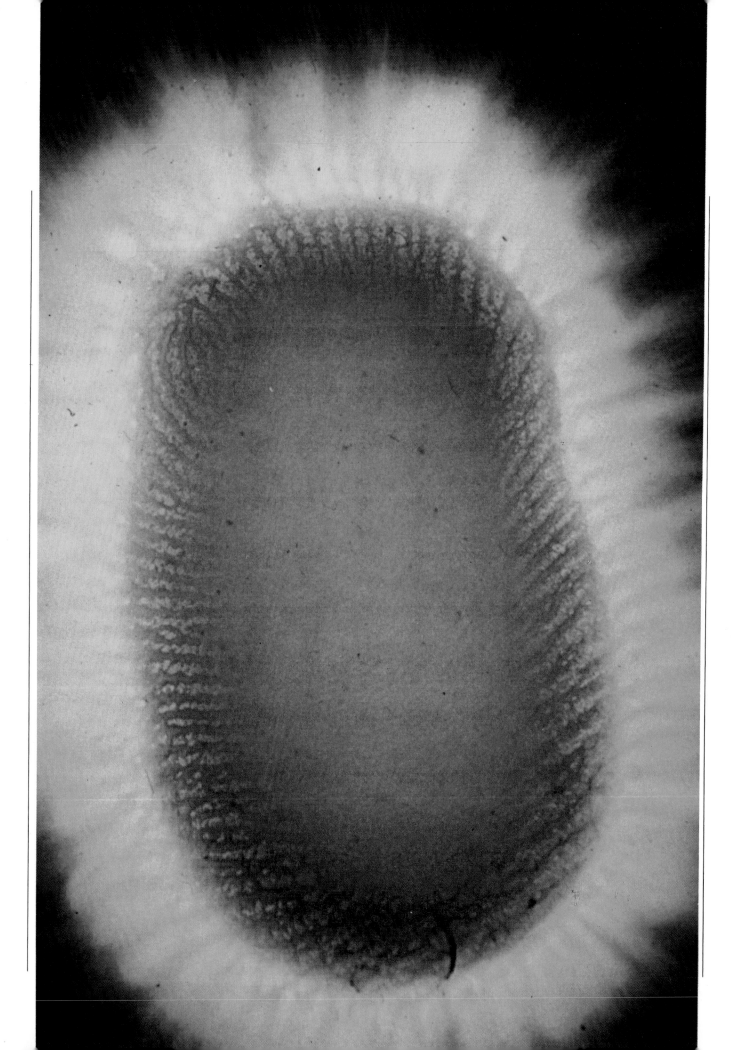

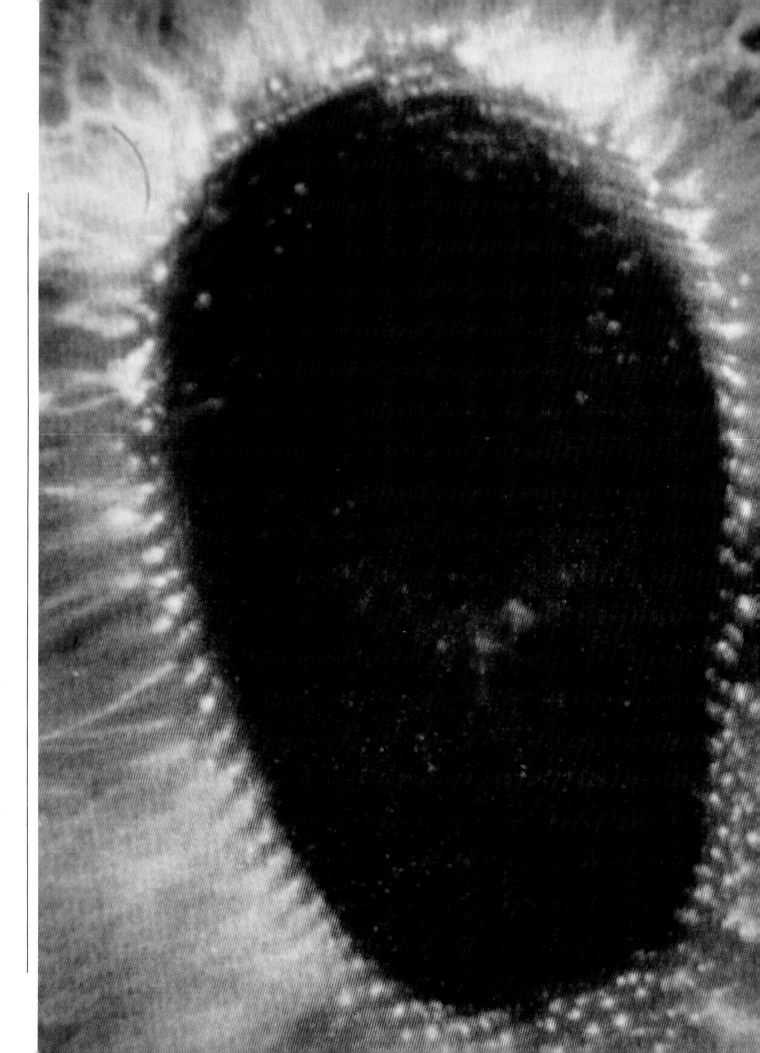

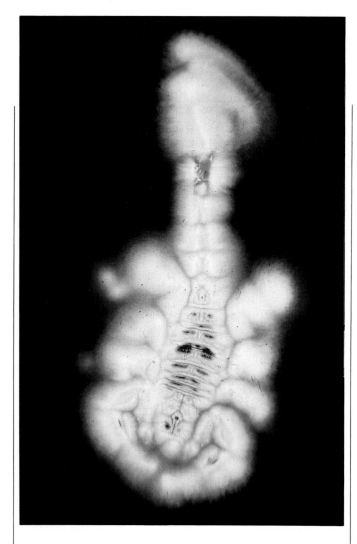

How important is this phenomenon? At one level it may be simply an interesting electrical effect: many of the activities of our cells and nerves involve electricity, and so it is hardly surprising that there should be a detectable electric field surrounding each of us or that it should show changes when we are in poor health. By contrast, believers in vitalism – the idea that living beings contain a certain vital principle absent from non-living objects – claim that the Kirlian aura is the visible manifestation of that vital principle.

The latter notion has led to some of the worst excesses of unorthodox medicine. For example, a 1960s 'therapy' called 'somatography' involved the therapist in massaging, not the patient's body, but his or her aura. Currently popular is 'therapeutic touch', in which the therapist runs the hands over the patient's 'life-field', a few centimetres away from the surface of the body.

Yet the aura must not be dismissed without question. The Christian habit of depicting glowing circles – haloes – over the heads of holy people dates back long before Christ, and

is found in many diverse cultures: it is reasonable to maintain that the halo is a representation of the aura. During the 19th century a number of perfectly respectable scientists made studies of the human aura and, interestingly, their results showed a remarkable degree of consistency. To take a single example, Dr Charles Féré wrote in the 1880s of seeing an orange glow around the head and hands of a patient who was suffering from hysteria. He described such glows as 'neuropathic auras', and there seems little reason to disbelieve his reports; he was a professional physician, and had no axe to grind.

Some specialists in the paranormal go further, however. They see the aura as being an 'etheric body', distinct from a person's physical body, and suggest that, for example, OOBEs are really cases of a person's etheric body travelling away from his or her physical body. This explanation is, on the face of it, somewhat foolish, yet perhaps it symbolizes the abilities of the rather 'larger-than-life' right-brain to do things that offend the sensibilities of our rationalist left-brains.

That living beings possess auras is something we can take as almost-proven fact. Exactly what those auras are is another matter altogether.

UPPER LEFT: a Kirlian photograph showing the aura of a living scorpion – much more colourful than the animal itself! **ABOVE:** *Kirlian photograph of a leaf.* **RIGHT:** *Long before the time of Christ, people regarded as holy were depicted with haloes, which were possibly representations of their auras; this picture, from the late 15th century, shows St Thomas à Becket, murdered in Canterbury Cathedral in 1170. It is possible, however, that the artists who created such pictures were rendering as visible something purely spiritual; we have all encountered genuinely saintly people who possess an 'aura' which we recognize even though we cannot see it.*

MAGIC

AUSTIN OSMAN SPARE, WHO died in 1956, was a self-styled magician; he was also a talented artist. On one occasion he was determined to show a visitor that his claims to arcane 'powers' were justified, and said that he would cause rose-petals to fall like snowflakes from the ceiling of his rather seedy lodgings. The spells were performed – and through the ceiling fell the lavatory, from the floor above.

Hardly rose-petals! Yet the coincidence was a strange one. Normally things do not descend from the average ceiling, be they rose-petals or lavatories, so the fact that *anything* happened in response to Spare's incantations is perhaps significant. Spare himself thought that his magical powers came from spirits which lived in 'spaces beyond space', as did the bizarre images he captured on paper. More probably, he was tapping the powers of his right-brain, which aided his artistic creativity while at the same time allowing him to perform apparently impossible acts.

Magicians like Spare, Aleister Crowley and others have relied on sexual magic. Their notion has been that, at the moment of orgasm, one can somehow attain, if only temporarily, a higher 'plane', and that this condition allows one to perform various occult deeds. Well, it sounds like a good excuse for having an orgasm.

Yet there may be something in the idea, if only because at the time of orgasm our rationalist left-brains are usually 'switched off'. Perhaps the moments in which our right-brains dominate are indeed times when we can enter a paranormal state.

Whatever the case, the embarrassing thing about various forms of magic is that they appear to work. The anecdote about Spare can be taken as an example of occidental, deliberate magic working – but not very well. Among primitive peoples, who accept such things rather than think about them, magic works very well indeed. Colin Wilson has cited a remarkable case in which a shaman of the South American tribe called the Calawayas believed that his wife was being unfaithful to him. No one could determine the truth or otherwise of his worry, and so it was decided to 'call the condor'. This huge bird is an important part of the Calawayas' world-view: they believe that human beings, on death, are reincarnated as condors. The unfortunate woman was staked out and, sure enough, from the skies a condor appeared: it strutted around for a while, and then made pecking motions towards the woman, an action assumed by

the tribe to be evidence of her guilt. A few days later the woman committed suicide.

We have to be careful about what we label 'magic' in this case. The unfortunate wife may have been totally innocent of adultery; she may have killed herself simply because all the rest of the members of the tribe ostracized her, believing in her guilt. It is, therefore, flaunting logic to suggest that the condor somehow 'knew' that she was an adultress. However, the strange part of the whole episode (which was recorded by a visiting television team) was that the condor appeared at all. Condors are not usually enthusiastic about human

ABOVE: *Aleister Crowley, the self-proclaimed Beast 666, in 1929. Crowley is certainly the most famous black magician of the 20th century – at least in the West – yet records of his magical feats are strangely lacking. His doctrine was: 'Do what thou wilt shall be the whole of the Law'. Opinions differed as to his personality; some regarded him as gifted but misled, others as a genius, and yet others as a figure of genuine evil. Today it is difficult to judge, because his system of 'magick' involved a high level of sexual activity – something extremely shocking in the earlier part of this century.* **RIGHT:** *Crowley as a young man.*

company, yet this one swooped from the skies to confront, not just a single human being, but a crowd of eager watchers; furthermore, it did so soon after being 'called'. Possibly this could have been coincidence, but if so the coincidence is an extraordinarily long one, especially since the Calawayas habitually find 'calling the condor' a useful way of sorting out disputes. One feels compelled to conclude that the rituals of the tribal elders did indeed 'call' the bird.

The evidence is overwhelming that primitive magic works, yet we in the developed hemisphere have an astonishingly poor record: people may delude themselves into believing that their magical acts have an effect, yet the results are ambiguous, to say the very least. Aleister Crowley is almost certainly the best-known magician of recent times, but when we look at his record of success we find a total blank. It is likely that magic simply cannot exist among the pre-conceptions of a technologically advanced society, that a society oriented entirely towards the development of left-brain faculties cannot, by its very nature, spawn people with magical powers. By contrast, a person brought up since infancy to believe that magical events are not only possible but an ordinary part of life is likely to develop paranormal powers. The important point is that, to the person concerned, those powers are in no way unusual; they are simply a fact of life.

RIGHT: In South Africa potions are made from bark and meat. The witchdoctor will smear the resulting mixture on himself and then administer it to the patient, to pass his power on for the desired cure or change to occur.
TOP: 'Doc' Shiels, a 'psychic entertainer' and artist famed in his native Cornwall, England, shows how easy it is to levitate people – in this case his daughter.
ABOVE: A ceremonial seal designed by J F C Fuller for Aleister Crowley.

PART TWO

PHYSICAL MYSTERIES

FORTEAN PHENOMENA

THE AMERICAN ECCENTRIC AND writer, Charles Fort (1874-1932), was no respecter of scientific orthodoxies: he 'collected', through his researches in the public libraries of New York, countless curious events which he described as the 'damned' – that is, cases which science rejected out of hand. Typical were newspaper reports of millions of frogs raining from the sky, people disappearing in front of witnesses, and flying saucers. His first two books, *X* and *Y*, remain unpublished; but his later works – *The Book of the Damned*, *New Lands*, *Lo!* and *Wild Talents* – created something of a sensation. (His earlier novel, *The Outcast Manufacturers*, failed to set the bookshops on fire.)

Fort presented the 'damned' in a higgledy-piggledy fashion and left it to the reader to decide what was going on. Sometimes, however, he felt moved to theorize. For example, his comment on the debate about whether an object can be accelerated move at a faster-than-light velocity was to question whether it had yet been proved that light actually *had* a velocity. Again, assuming that its craters were volcanic, he calculated that the moon was a mere 11,500 miles (18,500 km) from earth, and only about 100 miles (160 km) in diameter. It never crossed his mind that to explain the tides the average density of the 'mini-Moon' would have to be about ten times of solid lead. A further theory of his was that the earth does not rotate; on this he compromised, saying that it was possible that the earth rotated but, if so, it did so only about once a year.

Fort's theories are, then, the most palpable nonsense. But what about the mysterious events he dug out of the newspaper files in the New York libraries? Some of these have to be discounted out of hand. During the 19th century freelance newspaper-stringers in remote parts of the United States made a good living out of inventing improbable stories which would be featured in the major newspapers, whose editors were unable to check the truth because of the lack of adequate communications systems. Obviously, we do not know which of the stories were straightforward hoaxes and which were true (at least insofar as the reporters perceived them).

However, if only one of the stories collected by Fort was true, we have to re-examine our current understanding of the universe. It is not necessary to agree with Fort's hypothesis that there floats somewhere above the earth an invisible 'island' called Genesistrine, whose frogs, hazel-

nuts, etc., have a habit of leaping lemming-like over the island's edges to shower down upon us. It is, however, necessary to look objectively at the various reports of showers of frogs and hazelnuts – not just at the ones Fort came across in the press, but at the ones produced more recently.

In 1931, a year before Fort's own death, there was founded the Fortean Society (now known as the International Fortean Organization), a body dedicated to investigating the types of phenomenon reported by Fort. The names of the founders

TOP: *A 16th-century view of fishes falling from the sky.* **ABOVE:** *The original jacket of Charles Fort's Lo!, showing a shower of frogs.* **RIGHT:** *Charles Fort was a genius, whatever one might think of his writings, theories and frequent credulity. Here is the man himself, playing on the 'super checkerboard' which he devised.*

do not inspire confidence in the society's objectivity – Theodore Dreiser, John Cowper Powys, Ben Hecht and Alexander Woollcott among them – yet equally it cannot be denied that in the last couple of decades the Fortean Society, through its journal, *Fortean Times*, has exposed quite a number of unusual and unexplained things that orthodox science might rather choose to forget than explore. Indeed, the term 'Fortean phenomena' is now widely used to describe reported events that fly directly in the face of all perceived rationality.

Reports of frogs raining from the air are surprisingly numerous. As recently as 1973 *The Times* reported the showering of a French village, Brignoles, by untold numbers of frogs, and suggested that they had been swept up by a tornado and deposited many miles from home. This explanation seems improbable, since one would expect other elements of the frogs' environment – grass, leaves, etc., – to be swept up and deposited likewise. Earlier in the same year, a golf caddy in Arkansas had reported a similar event. The list of such reports is almost endless, and dates back to well before the time of Christ.

We have to remember that other things do 'incongruously' fall from the sky. It was in 1768 that the great French scientist, Antoine Lavoisier, was called in to investigate reports by peasants in the area of Luce that a huge stone had fallen from nowhere; Lavoisier's conclusion was that the peasants must be lying, because everyone knew that stones do not drop out of the sky. And in 1807 Thomas Jefferson came out with a famous comment: 'I could more easily believe that two Yankee professors would lie than that stones would fall from heaven'. Nowadays we know that stones – meteorites – do indeed fall from heaven, but we are less certain about the veracity of Yankee professors.

Fort was a particular devotee of reported showers of frogs, fishes and the like. However, it would be a mistake to

LEFT: *A woodcut from* Expositio Canonis Misse *(1496), by Bishop Odo of Cambrai. The scene purports to be the Israelites gathering the manna that has fallen from the heavens. Very Renaissance Israelites.* **ABOVE:** *A 1557 woodcut depicting a rain of crosses claimed to have occurred in 1503.*

assume that Fortean phenomena are all of this type: the range is vast. A notable Fortean phenomenon is spontaneous combustion – in which a person, for no apparent reason, catches fire. To judge by the remains of such unfortunate people, the flames are extremely hot, yet surrounding furnishings show little more than scorch-marks, if even that. For example, in 1966 a meter-reader in Coudersport, Pennsylvania, visited the house of a retired doctor, John Bentley, and discovered that the man had burned away completely except for the lower part of one leg. The flames had been so hot that they had burned a hole through the floor to the basement beneath; yet articles near to the site of the blaze remained virtually unscathed. In a case reported in the *British Medical Journal* in 1891 a

TOP: *Records of so-called 'Fortean phenomena' date back hundreds if not thousands of years before Fort's own lifetime; some regard the Biblical plagues of Egypt as early accounts of such phenomena. This print shows a rain of blood which, it is claimed, fell on France's Provence in July 1608.* **RIGHT:** *Another illustration from Olaus Magnus's* Historia de Gentibus Septentrionalibus *(1555). Clearly the author was enthused by showers of fishes.*

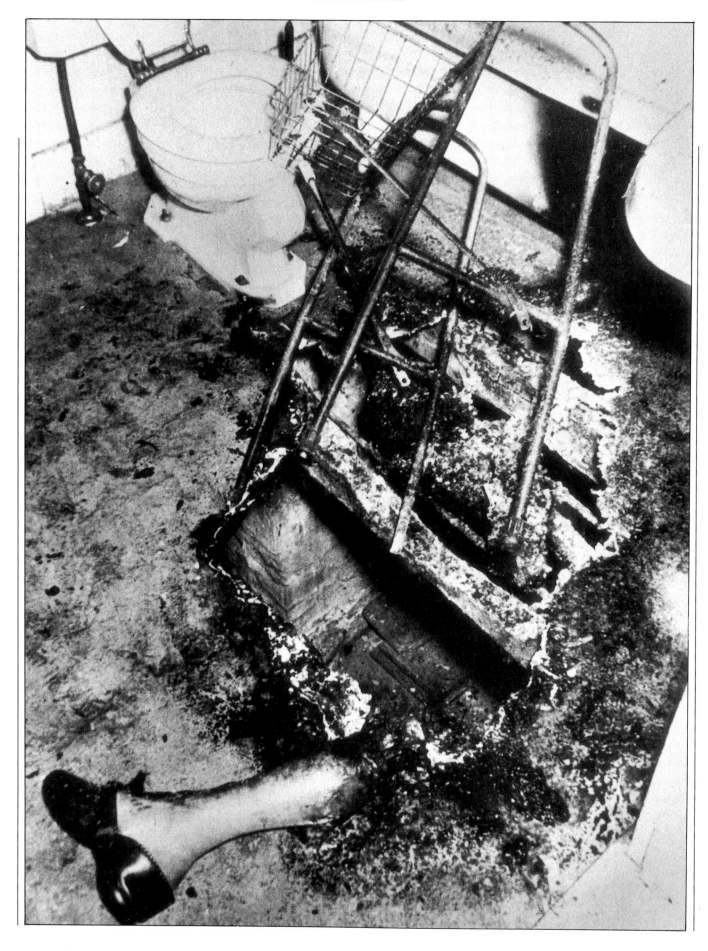

woman's legs were burnt to a crisp, yet the stockings she was wearing were unharmed. Fort reported the instance of the writer, J Temple Thurston, who in 1919 was discovered burned from the waist down, but whose clothing showed no trace of the fire. And in 1951 an elderly woman called Mary Reeser was found to have burned to death in a fire of such ferocity that all that remained were fragments; one grisly morsel was her skull, which had shrunk to the size of an orange, exactly the opposite of what normally happens when people burn to death. Once again, the effects of the fire were extremely localized – in this instance to Mrs Reeser and the armchair in which she had been sitting.

As yet, no one has been able to come up with any remotely plausible explanation for such phenomena as spontaneous combustion: a suggestion that ball lightning could be responsible has been flirted with, but generally rejected, and the charge that the victims were all drunkards, the alcohol in whose bloodstreams caught fire as they lit a cigarette, is unsustainable. This lack of any sensible explanation is characteristic of Fortean phenomena. It is possible to put forward theories about many of the physical oddities that have been reported – such as UFOs, which Fort himself recorded, although the term had yet to be coined – but, aside from Fort's own bizarre hypothesis, no one has yet been able even remotely to give any sort of rational explanation for showers of frogs or for people bursting spontaneously into flames. In fact, the problem is even deeper than it might at first appear: not only do we not know *how* these things come to happen, we have not the first idea *why* they should do so. From the point of view of physics, the events simply do not make sense; a religious person might suggest that God moves in mysterious ways, but a shower of frogs seems to have little religious purpose.

However, at this point we are drawn back to our discussion of the poltergeist effect (*see* page 44). There is no real point in throwing articles of furniture around the room, yet that is what poltergeists do. If, as seems most probable, poltergeist activity is the product of the right-brains of

people who are undergoing some mental trauma (typically pubescent girls), then is it not possible that the same people could be responsible for showers of frogs? It is widely reported in instances of poltergeist activity that, not only are existing objects thrown around, articles such as stones and needles seem to appear from nowhere. These items are seen not only by the person at the centre of the poltergeist event but also by onlookers.

Such notions are appealing, but in truth we are theorizing in a vacuum. A typical Fortean phenomenon remains just that – Fortean, or, in other words, totally inexplicable. Yet there are some types of event recorded by Fort which can, admittedly with some difficulty, be fitted into a rational framework. Sometimes the explanation is prosaic, as in the *Mary Celeste* mystery (*see* page 74) and sometimes it calls upon the assumed powers of the right-brain; yet in either case there is at least some sort of logic involved.

The same can hardly be said of a shower of frogs!

LEFT: *The remains of Dr John Bentley, who died on 5 December 1966 in Pennsylvania, presumably as a result of spontaneous combustion. Notice how the lavatory seat, which was highly combustible, has been totally unaffected.* **ABOVE:** *The great French scientist Antoine Lavoisier refused to believe in meteorites, the 'Fortean phenomenon' of the 18th century. However, the fact that Lavoisier was wrong should not compel us to believe in all accounts of strange falls from the skies.*

ABOVE: In July 1951 Mrs M H Reeser, of St Petersburg, Florida, was a victim of spontaneous combustion. Here workers clear the debris from her home. No one has yet been able to produce a convincing explanation for this phenomenon – neither paranormal researchers nor orthodox scientists – yet it certainly seems to occur. Perhaps, like ball lightning, it will one day be explicable in strictly rationalist terms, **LEFT:** An illustration published in the British Medical Journal in 1888 of an old soldier found dead of spontaneous combustion that year in a hayloft in Aberdeenshire, Scotland. **RIGHT:** The fall of the stars, as envisaged by Albrecht Dürer.

IN 1986 A YOUNG South American woman, temporarily living with her aunt near Taunton, England, seemed to disappear without trace. Her family were well off, and generated sufficient media publicity for reported sightings of the girl to come in from all over the British Isles. Family members followed up all these leads, but every time they seemed to be getting close to her the trail fizzled out. Finally, it was discovered that the young woman had run away from home and had been living the whole time in a Spanish convent. A less well off family might never have found her.

As many as 26,000 people disappear every year in the United Kingdom alone. Some are in due course found, having fled their homes for various reasons. Others are simply lost forever, and no explanation is forthcoming. In

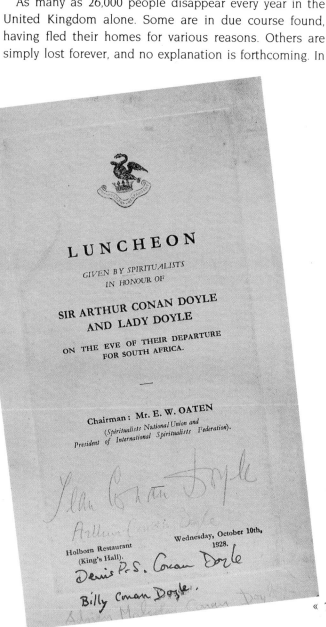

LUNCHEON

GIVEN BY SPIRITUALISTS
IN HONOUR OF

SIR ARTHUR CONAN DOYLE
AND LADY DOYLE

ON THE EVE OF THEIR DEPARTURE
FOR SOUTH AFRICA.

———

Chairman : Mr. E. W. OATEN

(Spiritualists National Union and
President of International Spiritualists Federation).

Holborn Restaurant   Wednesday, October 10th,
(King's Hall).   1928.

1978 a Devon schoolgirl, 13-year-old Genette Tate, was out on her bicycle delivering newspapers in the early morning. When she failed to return a search was mounted: her bicycle was discovered, but she never was – despite a vast and occasionally sensationalist campaign of media publicity mounted by her father. In 1969 a 14-year-old Norfolk girl, April Fabb, likewise disappeared while out cycling; once again, the bicycle was discovered but she was not. In both cases, it seems most probable that the unfortunate girls were abducted and murdered.

RIGHT: *Sir Arthur Conan Doyle is remembered not just as the creator of Sherlock Holmes and Dr Watson but as a researcher into spiritualism; in the photograph shown here the 'spirit of his mother' unexpectedly intruded.* **LEFT:** *Doyle's devotion to matters paranormal can be judged by this luncheon card. Before his death, he promised to communicate from beyond the grave – a promise that has yet to be kept.* **ABOVE:** *Doyle with his wife.*

Yet this may not necessarily be the case, for throughout the ages there have been persistent reports of people disappearing in curious circumstances and for no apparent reason. Many of the most frequently cited instances are in fact merely repetitions of hoaxes produced by 19th-century freelance newspaper-stringers. A certain Joe Mulholland was prime among these 'ornamentors of the truth', and he may have been responsible for the tale of the American farmer, David Lang, who famously disappeared in front of several witnesses in 1880. Later investigation has shown that neither Lang nor his farm near Gallatin, Tennessee, existed; yet the story is still told and retold.

The two classic cases of mysterious disappearances concern the ship *Mary Celeste* and the Bermuda Triangle. The *Mary Celeste* was found drifting in 1872. There was not a single person on board, yet clearly the ship had not been long abandoned – mugs of tea on the galley table were still warm, and the smell of tobacco smoke still lurked in the captain's cabin. Despite sensationalist accounts of the 'mystery', it seems certain that the passengers and crew for some unknown reason abandoned ship. Why else would the lifeboat be missing?

Many of the details of the 'accepted version' of the story can be traced to an anonymous short story published in the *Cornhill Magazine* in 1884. The author was Arthur Conan Doyle, who regarded his fiction, 'J. Habakuk Jephson's Statement', as a piece of harmless fun, and was horrified to discover that items such as the warm mugs of tea were now regarded as factual elements of the *Mary Celeste* story. (Doyle was also responsible for the popular misspelling of the craft's name as *Marie Celeste*.)

So why was the ship abandoned? There are various possible explanations. One is that the crew mutinied, murdered their captain, and then realized that it might be wise to flee the scene. Another, which is rather more probable, is that the people on the *Mary Celeste* and on the *Dei Gratia*, the ship which came across the abandoned hulk, had done a deal in order to claim salvage money. Whatever the case, it seems likely that there are very mundane explanations for the accident.

The myth of the Bermuda Triangle and the people who have 'disappeared' there barely deserves attention. It is a complete farrago. If one correlates the descriptions of various writers, the Triangle extends roughly from the Arctic to the Antarctic and from the Americas to Europe and Africa. The most famous Triangle case is that of Flight 19, a US

training flight which vanished in 'mysterious circumstances'. In fact the documentary evidence indicates quite clearly that all that happened was that the airplanes became completely lost and finally ran out of fuel far from land.

Yet there have been genuine instances of people disappearing. In 1809 Benjamin Bathurst stepped off his carriage at an inn in Perlberg, Germany, to enjoy a short rest, have some food and drink, and go to the toilet. He was seen to walk around to the other side of his horses, checking that they were in fit condition to continue; no one ever saw him again. In 1975 Mr and Mrs Jackson Wright were driving to New York through blinding snow; in the Lincoln Tunnel they agreed to pause and wipe snow from the front and rear windows. Jackson Wright never saw his wife, Martha, again.

In 1873 an English shoemaker called James Burne Worson disappeared into thin air in front of three of his friends between Leamington Spa and Coventry. Or did he? Paul Begg, one of the foremost authorities on cases of disappearing people, took the trouble to seek out the birth, death and marriage certificates of people living in the Leamington Spa area during the relevant period, and found no record of anyone called James Burne Worson. This may

(Gaspard Hauser.)

LEFT AND ABOVE: *The most famous case of someone appearing seemingly from nowhere is that of Kaspar Hauser, who arrived in Nuremberg in 1828 with no recollection of his previous existence. Five years later he died in violent circumstances that were as mysterious as his original appearance. Contemporary accounts of him varied; here we see him as both a civilized young man and a woebegone ragamuffin.*

mean that the tale is simply untrue; but there is another possibility, albeit not a very appealing one. Could it be that people vanish not just from this existence but also from the historical records? Clearly, by its very nature, this notion (to which, it should be stressed, Begg does not subscribe) cannot be taken any further, and its possibility is remote.

Of related interest is the phenomenon of 'appearing people', the classic case being that of Kaspar Hauser, a boy who suddenly turned up in Nuremberg in 1828. He could remember very little of his past, but recalled living in a small, confined room and being given only bread and water. The good citizens of Nuremberg adopted him, although there were a number of dissidents. In 1833 he was murdered – or, just possibly, he committed suicide. There is a possibility that the unfortunate Kaspar was the heir to the princedom of Baden, and was treated with gratuitous cruelty by a person keen to improve his or her chances of attaining the throne; however, this seems a trifle unlikely, because a quick murder would have been much more effective and much less likely to be detected.

Unpalatable though it might be, a case can be made for Kaspar Hauser's having in some way 'slipped through' from an alternate universe. Oddly, people are fairly scathing about the notion of alternate universes, despite the fact that they are indicated – although not proven – by modern physics. However, the reports of strange people appearing from nowhere are annoyingly persistent, and other explanations are, to say the least, inadequate. For example, the Englishwoman, Alexandra David-Neel, claimed to have created a person out of nothing (a *tulpa*) during a stay in Tibet; this *tulpa*, born from her deliberate will, was regarded as a real human being by other people, according to her account in *Magic and Mystery in Tibet*. It is hard to believe a word of it – but equally hard to believe she was lying.

There are numerous cases which suggest that people from alternate universes – and hence parallel earths – may somehow find themselves on this particular earth. A couple of examples will suffice. In 1905 a man arrested in Paris was found to speak a totally unknown language: he told the authorities, with obvious linguistic difficulty, that he was a citizen of a city called Lisbian, and rejected suggestions that by this he meant 'Lisbon'. And in 1851 the German authorities picked up Joseph Vorin, who claimed to come from the city of Laxaria in a country called Sakria.

All we can say is that the alternate-universe hypothesis is the least unpalatable of those on offer.

VAMPIRES AND WEREWOLVES

IT IS HARD TO establish quite how many young women were murdered in the early 1600s by the Polish countess, Elizabeth de Bathori, but the figure is generally regarded as lying somewhere between 300 and 650. Her motive for these murders was her desire to perpetuate her own beauty: she believed that bathing in the warm blood of the girls (preferably virgins) would preserve her own youthful appearance. Her methods of murder were, to say the least, unpleasant. She and the servants who had followed her repellent orders were brought to trial in 1611: thanks to our ancestors' customary notions of justice, the servants were burned to death while the countess was merely immured in her castle for the rest of her natural life.

A similar case had occurred nearly 200 years earlier, when the French aristocrat, Gilles de Rais, who had fought heroically against the English alongside Joan of Arc, was found to be responsible for the sadistic rape-murders of 150 or more children. He and his servants typically cut open the children's abdomens, so that he could view their internal organs while they yet lived; often he would sit, sexually aroused, on the stomachs of the children as they went through the final moments of their agonized deaths. Unlike the Countess de Bathori, Rais suffered the death penalty.

Both of these aristocrats – vile murderers or psychopaths, depending upon one's viewpoint – were vampires in that they gloried in the blood of other people. More than that, they actually *required* it. The political system of the day allowed them to perpetrate their crimes for extended periods, despite widespread rumours among the common people. Yet even today vampirism exists. Idi Amin, until 1979 dictator of Uganda, is widely reported to have sucked or eaten the internal organs of some of his murdered political opponents, and there are similar accounts of Haiti's 'Papa Doc', François Duvalier.

The classic vampire of stage and screen is of course Dracula, created in 1897 by Bram Stoker for the famous

Várrom Ruine Csejte

The prototype of Stoker's fictional Dracula was the real-life, 15th-century Walachian prince, Vlad IV, known as 'Vlad the Impaler', who was a military resistance leader. Curiously, he is in fact even now something of a cultural hero because of his military campaigns, yet he derived his nickname from his habit of dealing with prisoners-of-war by impaling them on sharp poles, reportedly deriving considerable enjoyment from watching them as they writhed helplessly in their death agonies. Whether he was a psychopath or a true vampire is impossible to determine.

Vampirism, from our modern viewpoint, is a psychological condition that is difficult to explain. For most of us, the thought of drinking warm human blood – or even, for that matter, animal blood – is enough to turn the stomach. Linking the experience with any erotic feeling whatsoever is likewise difficult. Yet there are people who find the practice sexually arousing – who *need* the experience.

horror novel. The reason the book was so successful was probably that Stoker, consciously or unconsciously, managed to put his finger on the undercurrent of eroticism associated with vampirism. This sexual element seems certainly to be present: the Countess de Bathori, although married, was certainly a lesbian deriving erotic pleasure as she bathed in the blood of her young female victims; Gilles de Rais, a rampant homosexual, vastly preferred that his victims be boys, although if necessary he would 'make do' with girls.

ABOVE: *Countess Elizabeth de Bathori, a woman who relied upon the blood of young girls in order – so she thought – to preserve her own youthfulness. The unfortunate girls were savagely tortured to death in order that the last drops of their blood could be extracted. The countess was finally tried for her disgusting crimes, and spent the last few years of her life immured in her castle* **LEFT. RIGHT:** *The letter-heading of The Dracula Society, whose founder members include film stars Christopher Lee, Peter Cushing and Vincent Price. The lettering is based on the style used in Romania during the 15th century, at the time of Vlad the Impaler.* **BACKGROUND:** *Gille de Rais' seal for his safe-conduct.*

The vampires of fable are of course rather different. They are not mentally disturbed murderers, but supernatural beings. They are 'living dead' who must sleep by day and venture abroad only by night. They are capable of changing their form from that of a human to that of a bat. They convert other people into vampires by sucking blood directly from their victims' jugular vein.

This image of the vampire is found throughout a surprisingly wide range of epochs and diversity of cultures, which has led many theorists to suggest that such bizarre creatures did in fact exist. However, we can see in the composite characterization a number of basic elements of folk-legends. For example, the ability of people, spirits or other entities to change shape on whim is an idea common to many primitive cultures: in the form of the shape-

changing phantom hitch-hiker, it is found even in the popular folklore of Western society. Likewise, the concept of the 'living dead' is found in many parts of the world – think of the zombies of the Caribbean – while tales of blood-sucking people or spirits can be traced back at least as far as the ancient Greeks.

LEFT AND RIGHT: *Nothing, it was believed, could prevent a werewolf having its wicked way with a human being, preferably a nubile female. Although wolves were indeed dangerous predators on human communities a few centuries ago in Central Europe, it is likely that legends about werewolves grew up for tribalistic reasons; a characteristic of tribes is that they are often keen to seek out scapegoats. What better scapegoat than a person accused of being able to turn into a wolf and savagely assault human beings? The bestial executions of so-called werewolves were matched only by those of women condemned as witches.* **ABOVE**: *Gilles de Rais – military hero and sadistic mass-murderer.*

All of these characteristics can be placed in the category of 'elemental fears'; that is, the very idea of them makes the average human being, whatever his or her cultural background, shudder. It is perhaps curious that to vampires has not been attributed the most frequently found 'elemental fear', the possession of feet 'fitted on backwards', a notion discovered in many folklores.

Werewolves – or, to be technical, lycanthropes – share with vampires many characteristics of folklore. They, too, are capable of changing their shape, and of course they use their supernatural strength to overpower and devour their victims. Here it would seem that popular fantasies about vampires have been grafted onto the dread felt for wolves – a dread that was very real, and far from foolish, in medieval Europe. Interestingly, it was widely believed that werewolves, on death, became vampires.

Another belief concerning werewolves was that, in their human form, they had a layer of hair underneath their skin; when they transformed themselves to become wolves, they simply turned their skin inside-out. This belief led to the slaughter of many innocent people, who were ripped open by ignorant mobs who believed they might be werewolves, and who sought proof. As with the contemporaneous witch hunts, which are more familiar to us, innocence did not save the unfortunate suspect from a particularly ghastly death.

It is improbable that there are or ever have been werewolves. But, as we have noted, vampires are still among us in the 20th century. Of course, they cannot get away with their activities on the same scale as did the Countess de Bathori – or perhaps they can. Between about 1910 and 1934 the American sadomasochistic maniac, Albert Fish, killed, raped and partially ate an untold number of children; he was caught only because he wrote a gloating letter to the mother of one of his victims. He confessed to killing some 400 children, although he was so insane by the time of his arrest that it is impossible to judge the validity of this. Over roughly the same period the so-called 'Monster of Düsseldorf', Peter Kürten, murdered and raped nine children, cutting their throats and drinking their blood. In prison awaiting his trial, he too wrote to the parents of some of his victims: the letters do not make enjoyable reading. He said drinking blood was to him as necessary a part of life as alcohol and cigarettes are to others. More recently, in the early 1980s, the London murderer, Dennis Nilsen, killed up to 16 young homosexuals whom he picked up in gay bars; his practice was then to dissect the body, cook it, and often eat parts of it. Reporters who have met Nilsen, a retiring civil servant, all agree that you could hardly meet a nicer man – the same was said of Fish and Kürten.

Clearly there is a relationship between vampirism and sex, and it is hard to escape the conclusion that this is because so many people – usually male – regard the sex act as an expression of dominance: we have phrases in the language such as 'sexual conquest', for example. Vampirism, involving the death and prior or subsequent sexual humiliation of the victim, is, from this viewpoint, the ultimate subjugation of another human being.

A further characteristic that must be noticed is the fundamental cowardice involved in vampiristic acts. As in cases of rape, most of the people we have noted were expressing their power over people who were utterly defenceless. The Countess de Bathori and Gilles de Rais had armies of servants to ensure that their unhappy victims had no chance of escape – and anyway they seem to have believed that their high positions in society would protect them from prosecution. Fish and Kürten preyed upon children. Although Nilsen picked on people his own size, he first of all poured enough alcohol into them to ensure that they had little chance of resisting his onslaught. (Those who did failed to report the event to the police because of fears that, as homosexuals, they might receive rough treatment.)

LEFT: *The belief in werewolves expressed through an early print showing one of the supposed monsters attacking a man. It may have been because wolves are intelligent animals that the idea that some of them were really humans in disguise sprang up.*

RIGHT: *The death of Gilles de Rais was not a pleasant one – yet it was far more merciful than what he had done to 150 or more children. Like Elizabeth de Bathori, de Rais revelled in the taking of blood; like her, he can be classified as a true vampire.*

PROCES CRIMINEL
DE MESSIRE GILLES
DE BRETAGNE BARON DE
RAIZ MARECHAL DE FRANCE
LEQVEL · FVT · EXECVTÉ · LE ·
20 OCTOBRE · 1440

Are vampires, as has often been suggested, people possessed by evil spirits? Such an explanation is facile, a fobbing-off of responsibilities on to the supernatural. Clearly vampirism is a psychological condition of which we as yet know little, created by social or genetic forces of which we as yet know even less. In general, we can note that vampires have suffered an 'over-parented' childhood – either they have been treated with excessive strictness or they have enjoyed a surfeit of pampering. However, this is almost certainly not the whole explanation.

Fears of the traditional vampire still survive. In 1973 a Polish expatriate, Demetrius Myiciura, was found dead in his flat in Stoke-on-Trent, England. He had choked to death on a clove of garlic which he had put in his mouth last thing at night; on his windowsill was a bowl of urine into which garlic had been mixed; salt had been sprinkled over his bed. Clearly Myiciura had been terrified of nocturnal vampiric attack. His death came about solely because of his terrors. Sadly, all too many children and young women have lost their lives because of the activities of genuine vampires.

LAKE MONSTERS

 DURING 1987 AN EXPEDITION searching Loch Ness, Scotland, picked up sonar traces of an object which the expedition members believed to be a fish or marine mammal; it was about the size of a large shark. The researchers dismissed suggestions that it might have been simply a rock, on the good grounds that, when they passed over the same area again later, the object was no longer there. They believed that they had finally come up with good evidence favouring the existence of the Loch Ness Monster – Nessie – although of course they had no means of telling what sort of animal Nessie might be.

There are a number of problems surrounding any claim that a huge creature dwells in the dark, cold waters of Loch Ness. The obvious one is that there cannot be just a single Nessie: there must be a whole extended family of them – in which case, why are sightings so rare? Another difficulty is that various observations of Nessie have differed quite dramatically from one another in their details: surely the loch cannot be populated by so many types of unknown animals!

A popular theory is that Nessie is a surviving plesiosaur, a marine reptile whose heyday, as with the other great reptiles, ended about 65 million years ago. The 1987 report might seem to support this hypothesis, because plesiosaurs looked much like dolphins, and dolphins of course look much like sharks. Yet there are again difficulties with this idea. For one thing, for a long period before about 10,000 years ago, Loch Ness, as a result of the Pleistocene Ice Age, was capped by a vast glacier. It would have been hard for any animal to have survived in the icy waters, even more so in

ice. This objection assumes, of course, that Nessie is not a comparatively recent immigrant: it is perfectly possible that a family of dolphins, whales or sharks accidentally found their way into Loch Ness a few hundred years ago and have dwelled and bred there ever since.

Photographs of Nessie abound, but few prove convincing on analysis. Some are definite fakes; others are not quite fakes, but are obviously not pictures of a monster – a much reprinted example would seem to show a 'monster' at most 20in (50cm) long, to judge by the pattern of the ripples surrounding the emergent head of the creature. (Almost certainly, this particular 'monster' was a water-bird.) Other pictures show logs floating downstream.

ABOVE: *A photograph taken at Loch Ness in 1933 by Hugh Gray is widely believed to show one of the animals thought to be resident in the lake. Gray's initial estimate was that the animal was about 40ft (12m) long, although he later modified this to 'very great'. Assuming that his recollection of its size is reliable, it is rather difficult to think what else this might be except the famous 'monster'.* **LEFT:** *The most famous of all the photographs purporting to show 'Nessie', this was taken in 1934 by the London surgeon R K Wilson. Conventional naturalists have proposed that the animal responsible was either a diving otter or a bird – in either case, a creature far smaller than the 'monster' is reputed to be.*

So, is there a monster in Loch Ness? The scientific evidence is poor, but reports from around the world – notably from North America – suggest that the idea is not so silly as it might seem. Numerous small lakes in Ireland are reported to have monsters; Lough Nahooin is one example. Lake Onegan, in British Columbia, apparently sports a creature called Ogopogo. Bear Lake, in Utah, is said to contain a monster, as is Lake Payette in Idaho. All are inexplicable.

It is possible that there is some connection between reports of lake monsters and sightings of UFOs – assuming that one believes in one of the psychological explanations of UFOs (*see* page 100).In the age when witches were credited with riding around the sky on broomsticks, people quite genuinely saw witches on broomsticks. Whether or not there was any objective reality in what they saw is a matter for debate. Similarly, now that we are all tuned in to the notion of visiting spaceships, people see what look like spaceships. It might well be that exactly the same mechanism is involved in sightings of monsters. Once a legend, for whatever reason, has come into existence, people will believe that they are likely to see monsters in that particular body of water and, purely because of their expectations, will actually do so.

Alternatively, of course, there may well be monsters in Loch Ness.

Jennifer Bruce, visiting from Vancouver in 1982, took a photograph of Urquhart Bay, Loch Ness **ABOVE**: At the time she noticed nothing unusual, yet a blow-up of the photograph **ABOVE RIGHT** reveals a traditional 'Nessie' head. It is obviously difficult to establish the scale of the creature in this photograph, but the resemblance between it and whatever it was that R K Wilson photographed (see page 83) is plain. **LEFT**: A claimed picture of Nessie shot by an anonymous photographer in September 1983. **RIGHT**: A model of Ogopogo on display at Kelowna, British Columbia.

BIGFOOT

IN 1970, IN NEPAL, two mountaineers, Don Whillans and Dougal Haston, came across a set of mysterious footprints at an altitude of about 13,000ft (4,000m). That night, Whillans was looking from his tent when he saw, some distance away in the moonlight, what seemed to him to be an ape-like creature moving on all fours. He could not make out any details.

Very few Europeans or North Americans have seen anything that might be the fabled Abominable Snowman, or Yeti, despite the fact that a number of expeditions have been sent from Europe specifically to track the mysterious beast down. A number of Westerners have *claimed* to have seen Yeti but, as John Napier has demonstrated in *Bigfoot*, the standard work on the subject, their accounts can be dismissed as misperceptions (or just plain hoaxes). The same is true of some of the celebrated photographs of animal tracks in the high Himalayas; the tracks can be seen to have been made by langurs, bears or even orangutans.

Yet a few of the photographs cannot be explained away so easily, and there is a powerful tradition among the Sherpas that there does indeed exist some kind of hairy humanlike creature in those mountain fastnesses. On the one hand, folk traditions often contain complete myths; on the other, the Sherpas obviously know a great deal more about the mountains than does any Westerner, and we should not dismiss their evidence out of hand. Moreover, there is corrobative evidence that a species of large, wild humanlike creatures may exist: there are several reports from North America of the Sasquatch, or Bigfoot, which is in many ways very similar to the Yeti. Clearly there is some link, either biologically or in terms of human psychology, between the two.

Here we shall take 'Bigfoot' to be the generic term for wild people, differentiating between the Asian Yeti and the North American Sasquatch. In addition, we have the humanlike Almas of the Soviet Union, Mongolia and China; an intriguing suggestion is that this latter might represent the last surviving relics of Neanderthal Man. Other areas of the world sport their own tales of wild races.

Thanks to the entertainment media, our popular perceptions of Bigfoot are muddled. Children may thrill to the thought that Bigfoot is implacably hostile and murderous, yet many of the traditions say quite the opposite, that Bigfoot is shy and frightened of human beings, which is precisely why it resides only in the most

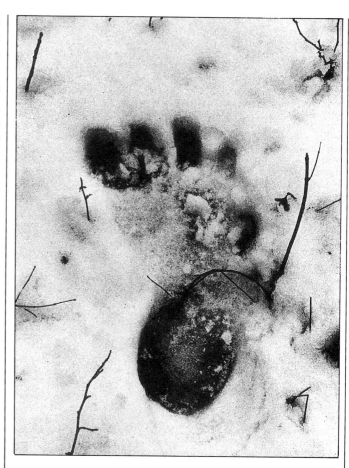

remote parts of the world. Another misconception is that Bigfoot is huge, towering above a human being; again, the various direct-encounter reports, when collated, show that the average height estimated is 5-6 ft (1.5-1.8 m) and sometimes much shorter. One can suggest that in fact Bigfoot is probably somewhat shorter than a normal adult human being, because observers of Bigfoots will almost inevitably exaggerate the dimensions of the 'monsters' they have seen. Both of these aspects would tend to support the hypothesis

RIGHT: *Paul Freeman, who claims to have seen a Bigfoot on 10 June 1982 in Umatilla National Forest, near Walla Walla, Washington State. In his right hand he holds a plastercast of the creature's footprint; in his left a painting of the Bigfoot's head.* **ABOVE:** *A footprint in snow, assumed to have been made by a Bigfoot, found at Bossburg, Washington State, in 1969. The footprint was over 16½in (42cm) long, and was one of over a thousand others found at the same time. Not too much credence can be attached to Bigfoot footprints found in snow; normal human footprints in snow can be vastly enlarged as the sun's heat melts the snow. However, it is rare for humans to run around in the snow in their bare feet!*

Several frames from the famous movie shot in 1967 at Bluff Creek, California, by Roger Patterson, apparently showing a female Bigfoot. Orthodox naturalists have analyzed this film and concluded that Patterson was being hoaxed. Others take the film to be genuine, and are militant in its support; the current writer has received lengthy and abusive transatlantic telephone calls protesting about his public expression of doubts over its veracity.

that Bigfoot might indeed be a survival of Neanderthal-type prehumans – exterminated, perhaps, by the more aggressive Cro-Magnon types in but all the most hostile regions. However, this is mere speculation: apart from anything else, we have no reason to believe that Neanderthal Man was hairy.

It is worth remembering at this point that there are other humanlike creatures that are frightened of human beings. For a considerable while reports of encounters with them in Africa were treated with derision in the West. The reference is, of course, to the gorilla, orangutan and the other large apes. It is perfectly reasonable to think that some of the apes may have a far wider range of habitats than we currently suppose. Moreover, there may be apes of which science as yet knows nothing. This may seem incredible, but remember that it was only a few decades ago that zoologists were smugly saying that every large mammal in the world was known to them – and then the okapi, which is about the size of a horse, was discovered.

If we accept that reclusive humanlike creatures exist, what do we know about their natures? First, the matter of their popularly-assumed ferocity. In this context, it is worth noting Don Whillans' testimony. He told the Sherpas on his expedition that he had seen a Yeti, and later he led them past the trail of footprints in the snow that he discovered. To his fascination, the Sherpas totally ignored them. His impression was that the Sherpas regarded the Yeti as a creature which, if you left it alone, would leave you alone. Far from being terrified of it, as so many sensationalist accounts would have us believe, the Sherpas instead display caution and respect towards it – much as we might regard a gorilla. The overall impression is that a Yeti might be dangerous if cornered, but otherwise need cause no fears.

This puts the Yeti into a rather different category from most other folk monsters, which are credited with rather nasty habits, such as eating people. The same is even more true of the Almas, viewed by the peoples of Central Asia as a lesser form of human being, but in no way a malevolent one – indeed, if we are to believe the various accounts, people in those parts treat any Almas they come across rather as one might treat a friendly dog one met in the street. These attitudes towards the assumed wild people tend to make one believe that the peoples of the various parts of Asia from which encounters have been reported are indeed telling the truth, rather than, as has so often been suggested, telling a good tale for the benefit of Western visitors.

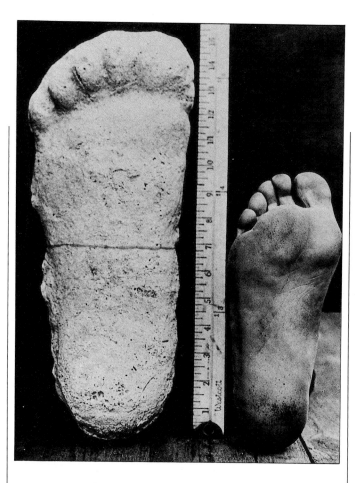

The Sasquatch is, as it were, the North American branch of the family. It is, of course, only fair to say at once that sceptics have considerable doubts about the very existence of the Sasquatch – doubts shared by some, but far from all, of the general public.

For example, in Skamania County, Washington State, it has been thought necessary to set a fine of $10,000 as punishment for the crime of killing a Sasquatch. As yet, no cases have come to court, and it is reasonable to assume that that none ever will and that the whole affair was intended more to attract tourism than as a piece of meaningful legislation.

To date the most famous appearance of a Sasquatch has been in an amateur film taken by Roger Patterson. In the

ABOVE: *A human male foot compared with a cast made after Roger Patterson's sighting of a supposed Bigfoot in 1967.* **RIGHT:** *Bob Gimlin, Roger Patterson's companion, displaying plastercasts made by the alleged Bigfoot which Patterson had filmed. the footprints were 14½in (37cm) long.* **FAR RIGHT:** *Bigfoot investigator René Dahinden beside a sculpture of Bigfoot created by Jim McClarin at Willow Creek, California.*

autumn of 1967 he was out riding with a friend in northern California when a female Sasquatch suddenly emerged from the trees ahead of them. Patterson's horse immediately threw him, but luckily he was still clutching his cine camera and had sufficient presence of mind to shoot some film – around 20-23 ft (6-7 m) – as the creature rather lazily ran off. This film has been shown countless times over the years, and has on occasion been analysed by professional naturalists.

The verdict returned by the naturalists is rather depressing. Although the creature is quite apparently a female (it has clearly visible breasts) its gait is like that of a man. It has pronounced human-like buttocks, unlike the apes. Foot-size and stride-length do not match up (although obviously such a judgement involves preconceptions as to the relationship between the foot-size and stride-length). Damningly, its stride, as can be seen from the film, is more like that of someone attempting to make their strides as long as possible than that of a creature moving naturally.

The inevitable conclusion would seem to be that

Patterson's film was a hoax. However, there is a problem here: Patterson was most manifestly convinced that what he filmed was exactly what he saw. The various researchers who have interviewed him are unanimous that he is utterly genuine about this. The only possible explanation – unless the naturalists, not all of whom are unsympathetic to the notion that the Sasquatch may exist, are wrong about the evidence of the film – is that Patterson himself was the victim of a hoax. This seems quite possible, since the top half of the filmed creature is, overall, bigger and bulkier than the bottom half would suggest it ought to be: such a creature would be a quadruped rather than a biped. One could guess – although one might be quite wrong – that Patterson's companion, Bob Gimlin, set up the incident. In the words of one naturalist who has commented on the affair, Bob Gimlin was 'somewhat of a "third man" character in this affair'. However, it should be stressed that it is far from proven that there was any hoaxing involved: unknown animals, almost by definition, will break some of the general rules inferred by naturalists from their observations of known animals.

Even if Patterson's film was the product of a hoax, a single piece of trickery does not mean that *all* stories of the Sasquatch are fallacious. A very convincing piece of evidence comes from an encounter in 1917 between an

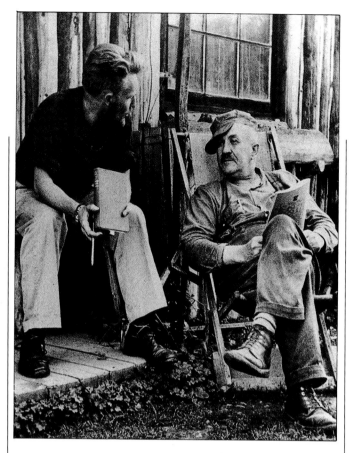

expedition led by a Swiss geologist, François de Loys, and a couple of large primates on the Venezuela/Colombia border. The primates were aggressive towards the humans, screaming shrilly and eventually defaecating into their own hands so that they could hurl excrement – a typical aggressive response of the larger primates. Finally the humans, who were terrified, shot at the male, although in fact it was the female that they killed (the male ran off).

The humans photographed the corpse, and from the photograph we can deduce that the primate was of the order of 5 ft (1.5 m) tall. De Loys himself measured the height as 5 ft 1¾ in (1.57 m), which certainly put the creature firmly into the height-range of adult human beings – and, likewise, meant that it was far larger than any known New World primate. Moreover, the size of the forehead and the dentition indicated that this creature was only remotely, if at all, related to the known primates of the Americas; and its overall appearance is definitely humanoid. At least one naturalist has suggested that the creature represents an advanced ape, evolving independently in the Americas, of roughly the same status as *Pithecanthropus erectus*.

Or, perhaps, the primate concerned was actually a member of a surviving colony of primitive human beings (such as *Pithecanthropus*), living advisedly far from *Homo sapiens* in the least-travelled parts of Latin America? This is far from beyond the bounds of possibility. However, there is one interesting point. The creature in de Loys' photograph,

while definitely female, has the flat breasts typical of apes. By contrast, the female Yeti are widely reported by the Sherpas to have breasts so huge and droopy that they have to throw them back over their shoulders in order to run. It is likely that the Sherpa tales are, in this respect, exaggerated; but nevertheless the very fact that the exaggeration should be promulgated suggests that Yeti females have, like their human counterparts, protuberant breasts. They are, therefore, a long way – speaking in terms of evolution – from the gorillas, chimps, orangutans and other higher primates. They are much more like us.

The photograph taken by de Loys' expedition provides virtual proof that unknown anthropoids dwell in the Americas, and so it does not seem too ridiculous to believe that at least some of the reported Sasquatch sightings are perfectly genuine. One of these days a live Bigfoot may be, however unwillingly, brought to meet its more 'advanced' fellows, although in a way one hopes that this never comes about. Bigfoot may not have developed a technology capable of curing killer diseases and manufacturing digital watches; on the other hand, it has yet to invent nuclear warfare.

Let us hope that, should the existence of Bigfoot finally be proved, we treat our 'fellows' humanely, rather than hunt them down and exterminate them as, for example, the Europeans destroyed the indigenous Tasmanians during the 19th century. Perhaps Bigfoot is wise to hide in the remote parts of the world.

There are, then, several possible explanations of the Bigfoot mystery. Since the reports from different parts of the world vary quite dramatically in their details, it is quite possible that all of the explanations may be correct, and that attempts to produce a unified theory are born from the human impulse to rationalize things. There could be a reclusive culture of hirsute humans in the high Himalayas *and* unknown species of primates in South America; we may simply be compounding several mysteries into one.

ABOVE: *Albert Ostman, on the right, being interviewed by John Green. Ostman claimed that in 1924 he had been abducted by a family of Sasquatches in British Columbia. Despite the apparent implausibility of the tale, and the fact that he waited until 1957 to tell it, circumstantial details of his account have convinced many people who are normally sceptics that he was indeed telling the truth.* **RIGHT:** *The corpse of a strangely manlike animal killed by François de Loys and his party on the Venezuela/Colombia border in 1917. This creature is unknown to science. It is impossible to determine whether it is an ape or a hominid.*

LITTLE PEOPLE

BETWEEN 1917 AND 1920 two young girls, Frances Griffiths and her cousin, Elsie Wright, took a series of astonishing photographs in a 'fairy glen' at the back of Elsie's house in Cottingley, Yorkshire. These photographs purported to show the girls playing with elves and fairies – who came complete with wings and merry expressions, just like the fairies in Victorian children's books. Sir Arthur Conan Doyle, whose interest in matters psychic was intense, publicized the case, and since then the 'Cottingley Fairies' have become established in the literature.

It is still said that no scientific test has been able to prove that these photographs were faked. This is curious, because merely by looking at them you can see sufficient discrepancies of focus and perspective to indicate that the 'fairies' are paper cut-outs. This the two hoaxers admitted themselves in later life.

A further reason for doubting the photographs had always been that the idea of fairies as ethereal miniatures is a comparatively recent one. The little people – elementals – were traditionally regarded as something rather different: they were troglodytic spirits, about the size of a 10-year-old human child, and far from being friendly and playful they could be very unpleasant indeed, if crossed. They possessed formidable spiritual powers, and some varieties had

exceedingly nasty habits; for example, redcaps got their name because of their practice of dying their caps in travellers' blood. Leprechauns and brownies, who are positively helpful to human beings, are very much in the minority.

A number of writers have linked fairies to the UFO phenomenon. Some have taken a 'physical' approach, suggesting that all the traditional tales of fairies are really accounts of the activities of visiting Little Green Men. Others have suggested, as we have seen in connection with lake monsters (*see* page 82), that each age and culture produces its own supernatural object which observers are capable of reifying, or, at the very least, of *believing* that they see. (The distinction between the two latter hypotheses may be an artificial one, if we are to take at face value some of the ideas of modern physics.)

Another theory is that there genuinely did coexist with humanity a race of smaller, humanoid, intelligent creatures, and it is very tempting to suggest that this might be a product of the experiences of our Cro-Magnon-type ancestors with the surviving remnants of Neanderthal-type humans. Of course, folk-memories do last a long time, and so the theory cannot be thrown out completely. However, like so many superficially attractive ideas, it suffers from a complete lack of supporting evidence.

Do fairies exist? Alternatively, did they exist in historical times, but have now died out? This is a genuine mystery, and one that may never be solved. However, it seems likely that the 'physical' explanation is erroneous, in that no one has yet unearthed a fossil fairy. Or is the belief in little people a necessary part of the human psyche? It seems that most of us have to believe that the universe is, as it were, made up of 'us' and 'them', and fairies are good candidates for 'them'.

LEFT: AND RIGHT: *Two typical examples of the faked series of 'Cottingley Fairy' photographs. Surprisingly, these pictures for decades hoodwinked otherwise sober individuals.* **UPPER LEFT:** *A fairy ring, as depicted in Olaus Magnus' Historia de Gentibus Septentrionalibus, 1558. The depiction of the 'little people' could hardly be more different from that in the 'Cottingley Fairy' forgeries, which were a product of the romanticized image of fairies generated during the Victorian era. Here the emphasis is both animalistic and sexual; note the juxtaposition of a serpent with the fairy at* **TOP LEFT.** **BACKGROUND:** *Fairies dancing, from an old English Chapbook.*

MIRACLES

IN MAY 1917 THREE young children were looking after sheep near Fátima, Portugal. The three had not long gone through the rosary when, after a few flashes of lightning, the Virgin Mary appeared before them. She asked the children to return to the site on the 13th of each month until October of that year, at which time she would tell them why she had come. On the next appointed day, 13 June, about 60 people were with the children, and they saw very little, although the eldest child, Lucia Santos, held a deeply religious conversation with an invisible entity. On being asked if the three children would soon be escorted to Heaven, the entity said that Lucia's two companions, her cousins Francisco and Jacinta Marto, would indeed shuffle off this mortal coil in the near future, but that Lucia herself would remain on earth for some while longer. (This proved to be true: thanks to the great influenza epidemic of 1919, Francisco died in that year and Jacinta in the following one, yet Lucia lived to a ripe old age.)

The meeting on 13 July was attended by a crowd of about 5,000, and that in August by about 20,000. The latter fell completely flat because the sub-prefect of the region had decided to imprison the children for the relevant day. However, on their release, the children had a vision of the Virgin on the 19th day of the month; this time the Virgin said that the promised October revelation would be rather less than expected, because of the failure to keep up the meetings on each 13th day of the month, but that it would still be fairly sensational; she also requested that the children pressurize for a chapel to be built.

RIGHT: The three children at the heart of the Fátima miracles. From left to right, they are Jacinta, Francisco and Lucia. BELOW: A selection of the crowd viewing the reported solar phenomena witnessed at Fátima on 13 October 1917.

Along came 13 September, and this time there were as many as 30,000 spectators present. Some were disappointed, seeing nothing except Lucia talking to empty air, but others noted rose-petals falling to the ground and the presence of a curious ball of light 'gliding', according to one witness, 'slowly and majestically through space'.

The apparition of 13 October was obviously going to be the big one, and no fewer than 70,000 people turned out to watch it. There was such a crush that the three children had some difficulty in fighting their way through to the meeting-place. Lucia conversed with the Virgin, and then saw the entire Holy Family in the sky, just next to the sun. She exhorted the crowd to look in that direction: according to about half of the observers, the sun then cavorted in a pinwheel fashion around the sky. The other half of the crowd saw nothing of interest.

Lucia lived on to become a nun, and in her memoirs, fully published in 1942, she claimed several further supernatural encounters. There seems to be little doubt that she

genuinely believed in her visitations by members of the Holy Family; yet, equally, it seems unlikely that it happened. Moreover, although there were countless press photographers present at the final Fátima vision, not one of them seems to have been moved to photograph the sun jumping around the sky. (A much-reproduced picture is actually of an earlier solar eclipse, and was taken in a quite different part of the world.)

Whatever went on in the mind of Lucia Santos in 1917, we can describe the whole series of events as being, together, a miracle. But what exactly do we mean by the word 'miracle'? One dictionary provides as a definition 'a marvellous event attributed to a supernatural cause'. This hardly helps us explain miracles; slightly to pervert a statement of Arthur C Clarke, any effect produced by a technology beyond our comprehension is, by definition, miraculous, so that merely to ascribe miracles to the 'supernatural' is to dodge the issue, rather as if we said 'it's all done by physics'.

Yet miracles do seem to occur. Sai Baba of Puttaparti is probably the most 'miraculous' person of the 20th century. Whereas other yogis perform miracles only occasionally and often in dubious circumstances, Baba executes wonders on the large scale, often in front of teams of respectable witnesses or vast crowds of ordinary believers. Moreover – that rarest of things in the supernatural world – he performs his miracles on demand.

According to various reports, Baba can materialize objects from nowhere, levitate, perform acts of psychokinesis, and display many other startling abilities. At his ashram, close by Puttaparti, thousands throng every year to see him at work. Most of his miracles are connected with healing. His most astonishing reported feat to date is the raising of a young man from the dead. In fact, it is claimed that he has done this several times, but only once has the miracle been performed under stringent scientific checks. Interestingly, Baba claims to be an avatar, meaning that he has roughly

the same relation to the deity as did Jesus Christ; one of Christ's most famous miracles was the raising of a young man, Lazarus, from the dead.

Baba is a healer and psychic surgeon, too. The Tasmanian journalist, Howard Murphet, in his biography, *Sai Baba: Man of Miracles*, tells of a number of instances in which he personally watched Baba at work. In one well attested case Baba was able to cure a patient suffering from terminal cancer – although this is perhaps less miraculous than some of his other feats, in that cancer is almost certainly at least partly psychosomatic.

Baba is, apparently, a cheerful fellow, and welcomes visitors – even sceptical ones – with smiles and jokes. Unlike many other assumed miracle-workers, he does not refuse to prove his abilities in front of cynics: often he will produce for them a handful of sacred ash which he has materialized before their very eyes. To others he gives photographs of himself from which, from time to time over succeeding years, sacred ash will spontaneously materialize.

Of course, it is impossible to produce even tentative explanations of miracles: by definition, they are inexplicable. Moreover, the two types of miracle discussed here are vastly different – Lucia's religious visions are, quite literally, a world away from Baba's materializations and levitations. All we can say is that the latter type of miracle seems to have a lot in common with psychokinesis (*see* page 36). The former is certainly outside the province of any form of scientific investigation.

Images of the Virgin Mary are widely reported to move, weep and generally perform miracles. **TOP LEFT:** *A statue of the Virgin, blood pouring from her eyes, photographed in 1972 in Porto San Stefano, Italy,* **LEFT:** *A 1984 photograph, taken in Brooklyn, New York, of a statue of Mary apparently weeping. It goes without saying that conventional science has no explanation for such phenomena – assuming that is, that they are not hoaxes.* **ABOVE RIGHT:** *Sai Baba of Puttaparti – a man for whom, if all accounts are to be believed, miracles are everyday occurrences. Witnesses of his deeds have included many highly reputable people, who are unlikely to have clubbed together to spread a hoax. It is difficult to equate some of Baba's feats – such as raising a person from the dead – with our everyday notions of 'common sense'.*

UNIDENTIFIED FLYING OBJECTS

THE ROMAN HISTORIAN, LIVY (59BC-AD17) seems to have been a great enthusiast for celestial happenings, for he recorded about 30 unusual things observed in the skies. It seems unlikely that he himself saw any of these – most had occurred long before his time – yet the accounts he gives could, with only minor changes, be mistaken for modern UFO reports. For example, he describes how skyships were witnessed in 218BC and how, four years later, a vision of men in white clothes gathered round an altar was seen in the skies over Hadria.

Generally speaking, the history of UFOs is traced back to 24 June 1947, when a pilot called Kenneth Arnold was flying his private plane near Mount Rainier, in Washington State, and saw nine gleaming discs swooping in and out of the peaks of the Cascade Mountains. He later described the motion of the discs as being much like that of a saucer 'skipped' across water; and the term 'flying saucer' was born. But reports of UFOs go back long before that, as we have seen. There is even claimed to be one in the Old Testament, in *Ezekiel*:

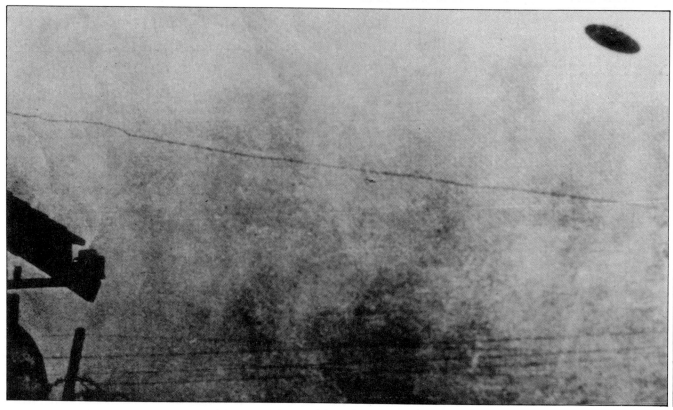

... a stormy wind blew from the north, a great cloud with light around it, a fire from which flashings of lightning darted, and in the centre a sheen-like bronze at the heart of the fire. In the centre I saw what seemed four animals. They looked like this. They were of human form. Each had four faces, each had four wings. Their legs were straight; they had hooves like oxen, glittering like polished brass. Human hands showed under their wings; the faces of all four were turned to the four quarters. . .

This is startling stuff, but it seems that the 'spaceships of Ezekiel', written up so enthusiastically in the media, owe their origins to nothing more than a particularly fanciful description of a rare atmospheric effect, whereby an observer looking sunward sees four 'sundogs' (parhelia) spaced regularly in a ring around the sun.

Every age seems to have its own version of UFOs. Long ago, people quite genuinely believed they saw witches flying through the skies on broomsticks. During the winter and spring of 1896-97 there were widespread reports of an airship flying over North America; it took about five months

LEFT: *A photograph taken in May 1951 by the Trent family of McMinnville, Oregon, showing the UFO which they observed. This is one of the very few UFO photographs to have passed all scientific tests – including recent examinations using computer enhancement.* **ABOVE LEFT**: *Kenneth Arnold.* **ABOVE**: *The Spring 1948 issue of Fate – the very first edition of the magazine – showed an illustration of Arnold's encounter that relied considerably on artistic licence.* **RIGHT**: *One of the rarer of the dozens of photographs produced by George Adamski, showing a cigar-shaped 'mothership' and several 'scout craft'. Most modern ufologists believe that this, like others produced by Adamski, was a fake.*

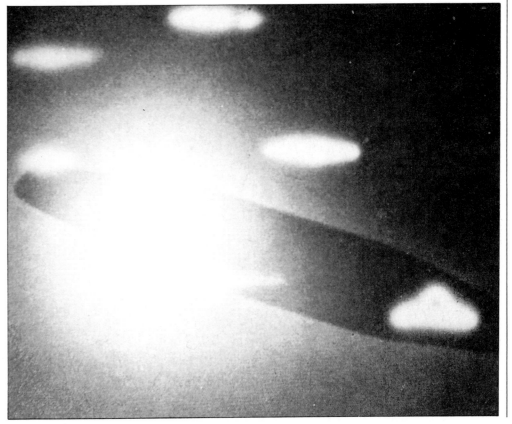

to cross the country from west to east. In terms of cultural history, this case is particularly interesting, because in 1896 the airship had roughly the same status in the popular consciousness as the spaceship has today: you know they exist, but you would be mighty surprised to see one.

It is true that a great deal of nonsense is talked on the subject of UFOs. For example, in 1975 Marshall Herff Applewhite and Bonnie Lu Trusdale Nettles, generally known as 'Bo' and 'Peep', told the world that they had come to this planet by UFO from 'the level above human'; their objective was to enlist as many humans as possible in 'the Process' and then to return, with these acolytes, to the 'higher level'. A notable point was that, if you wanted to join 'the Process', all you had to do was to hand over all your worldly goods to Bo and Peep. These two worthies claimed that within about six months their physical bodies would be assassinated, but that their spirits would live on to guide their disciples skywards. As many as 1,000 people at any one time believed this stuff, although after Bo and Peep failed to be assassinated on schedule the numbers dropped off.

Various UFO photographs, all probably fakes. **LEFT AND RIGHT:** *In 1963 and 1966 Paul Villa claimed that he chatted with alien astronauts who arrived in these two discs. Perhaps they should have let their tentacles do the walking.* **ABOVE:** *A spinning UFO photographed in Oregon in 1964: all resemblances to a light fitting are totally coincidental.* **TOP FAR RIGHT:** *A claimed UFO photographed in 1954 in Coniston, Cumbria, England.* **TOP RIGHT:** *A claimed UFO photographed in 1952 in Passiac, New Jersey.*

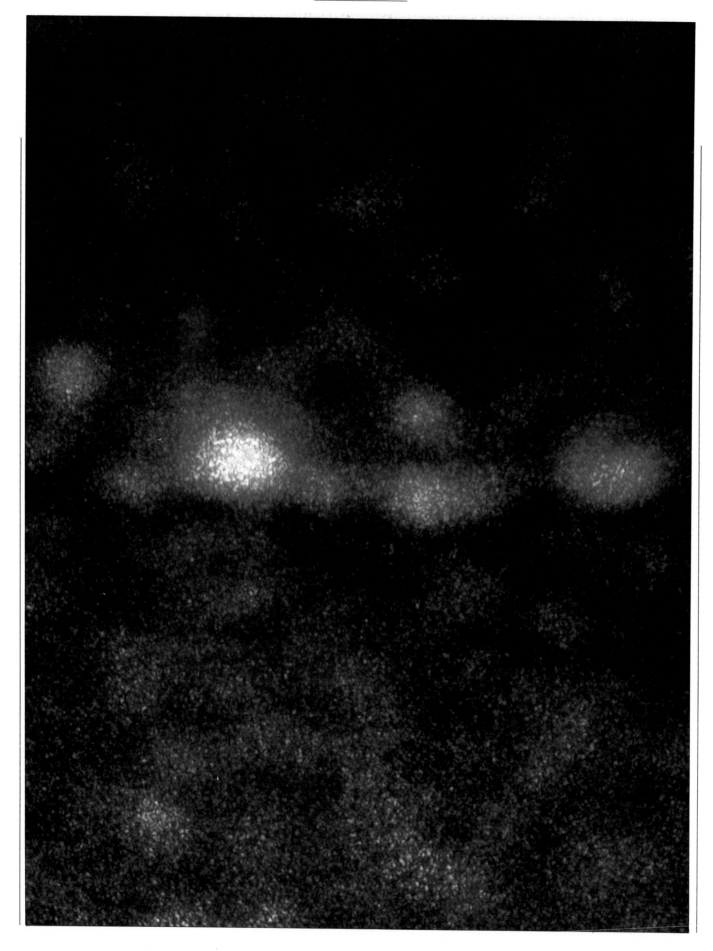

UFO hoaxes abound. A deliberate spoof, *An Account of a Meeting with Denizens of Another World, 1871* (1979) by 'William Loosley', has been quoted as genuine by the credulous, as has *Flying Saucer from Mars* (1955) by 'Cedric Allingham'. T. Lobsang Rampa, the famous Tibetan sage and author of books such as *The Third Eye* (1956), otherwise known as the Irish hoaxer, Cyril Hoskin, tells us the Revealed Truth. UFOs are actually spaceships visiting from a world made out of antimatter. This is why they never touch down: matter and antimatter explode with colossal ferocity on contact. The trouble with Rampa's explanation is that air, too, is made out of matter.

Moreover, there are quite a few reports of UFOs touching down. The most famous concern the claims of Californian soft-drinks salesman, George Adamski, who had a number of 'close encounters'. Much of the associated evidence suggests that Adamski was either very imaginative or, shall we say, an entrepreneur. However, there are two follow-ups to Adamski's story that are little known, and both are interesting.

First, 24 hours after Adamski's death in 1964, a man called Edward Bryant was walking in open country in Devon, England, when he came across a 'parked' UFO. One of the aliens from the craft, an individual with a boyish appearance, introduced himself to Bryant as 'Yamski' and asked Bryant to give his regards to 'Des' or 'Les'. Now, it was unlikely that Bryant could have heard of Adamski's death by the time of his alleged encounter. Moreover, according to Adamski's first co-author, the journalist, Desmond Leslie ('Des' or 'Les'?), only he and a few others knew that the ufonauts had promised Adamski that he would on death pay a speedy return visit to earth in the form of a young boy.

Unfortunately, Bryant failed to tell his story until some weeks later, by which time the whole affair had become a lot less miraculous. At least one ufologist who worked on the case was convinced that Bryant was lying, and his partner in

LEFT: *Modern, scientific ufologists have little brief for tales of abductions by extraterrestrials, instead regarding the various phenomena as having diverse sources. This photograph shows an example of a UAP (unidentified atmospheric phenomenon) witnessed in a remote Norwegian valley at Hessdalen, near the Arctic Circle. These blobs of light appear repeatedly in the valley, yet various scientific expeditions have failed to determine their origin or nature. That the lights exist is proved by the countless photographs of them which have been taken. As to what they are, no one yet has a clue.* ABOVE: *Jenny Randles, one of the most widely respected ufologists of modern times. Her objectivity has earned the regard of even convinced sceptics.*

the investigation, although more sympathetic, was careful to point out that the possibility of Bryant inventing the story was a very real one. Sadly, Bryant died only a couple of years after his alleged encounter, and so we cannot ask him.

The second curious follow-up to the Adamski case occurred in 1980, with the discovery in northern England – Todmorden, West Yorkshire, to be precise – of the body of a man. This man had disappeared some days earlier. His trousers were ripped, and his shirt was missing. He had some superficial cuts on his hands and knees and a scrape on his right thigh. Perhaps more significantly, he had a curious burn-mark on his head – it seemed to be an acid burn – which, according to the post mortem, had occurred some two days before his death and appeared to have been treated with some form of ointment. The man had not been living as a tramp during the time between his disappearance and the discovery of his corpse: for example, he had only a one-day stubble, despite having been missing for five days.

The whole case is a mystery, and still no one knows for certain what happened. It also sparked off a UFO 'flap', for various understandable reasons. Jenny Randles, who has written the standard book on the affair, gives a chronology: on 6 June the man disappeared; on 7 June a huge ball of orange light was seen in the nearby city of Bradford; similar lights were seen in Todmorden itself and neighbouring Halifax on 8 June; on 9 and 10 June there were many reports

Some of the more impressive UFO photographs are those where it was only later that the photographer noted the presence of a UFO. **LEFT**: Japanese news photographer Tsutomu Nakayama took this shot in Hawaii in April 1974, and only when it was developed did he notice the UFO. **TOP RIGHT**: Wilfred Power, had a very similar experience when he thought he was photographing nothing more than a giraffe at Plymouth Zoo, Devon, England. **ABOVE AND RIGHT**: Two frequently reproduced photograhs purporting to show flying saucers. One is probably of reflections of lights in the windows of the laboratory from which it was taken; the other is a lenticular cloud formation.

of celestial lights from the region south of Bradford; and on 11 June the corpse was discovered. The curious circumstances of the case, coupled with all this UFO activity, made it inevitable that UFOs would be related to the bizarre death. But there was a third factor: the deceased's name was Zigmund Adamski.

There is no suggestion that Zigmund was any relation of George, yet Adamski is not a common name in Great Britain. A curious coincidence, or something more? It is hard to tell. Yet it is worth noting that irritating little parallels like this one occur throughout the field of the paranormal.

Two UFO cases stand alone as the most widely reported of all. One is the Tunguska explosion of 1908 and the other is the 'interrupted journey' of Betty and Barney Hill in 1961.

The Tunguska forest is in a remote part of Siberia. Early on 30 June 1908 the few people of the region saw a fireball zooming through the air, leaving a trail of smoke and changing course at least once before exploding with a violence equivalent to about 20 megatons. Fortunately, because the region was – and is – so sparsely populated, few

if any people lost their lives, although the slaughter among the animal population was horrific. From the point of view of science, though, the remoteness of the area and the sparseness of population combined to ensure that 20 years were to pass before a scientific expedition from Moscow arrived. The scientists expected to find a meteoritic impact crater. Instead they found good evidence that the object had indeed, just as the peasants reported, exploded in the air. Vast areas of trees had been blown flat, all lying pointing outwards from the blast's obvious epicentre. The scientists discovered many other curiosities – although not quite so many as are listed in the more popular accounts of the affair.

BELOW: *Betty and Barney Hill, the two most famous UFO contactees of all time.*
RIGHT: *Each year between 1954 and 1977 alleged UFO contactee George Van Tassell organized the Giant Rock Convention in California; his claim was that the Giant Rock area naturally attracted UFOs. This photograph was taken in 1970 in the area by Reserve Sheriff W A Ackerman. The pedestrians seem surprisingly unconcerned by the apparition.*

The opinion of orthodox science is that the object which fell in 1908 was a very small comet. This would explain, for example, the curious discoveries of deposits of anomalous chemical elements at the blast's 'ground zero'. Also, it is perfectly possible that a comet, entering the atmosphere from the cold, unpressurized wastes of space, would explode before reaching the ground. It is *just* possible that, through differential ablation, the comet might change course as it soared through the skies.

However, in the late 1940s the idea emerged that the object might have been an extraterrestrial spacecraft, whose occupants, realizing that the machine was getting wildly out of control and that the engine was about to explode, succeeded in steering it to a remote part of the globe – either to spare human life or simply out of a desire for secrecy.

The case of Betty and Barney Hill is of special interest because it has been so widely documented: the standard book on the subject is John Fuller's *The Interrupted Journey*

(1966). In 1961 the Hills were driving home when they saw a light in the sky which they thought might be a UFO. They did not think too much about it until they reached home, when they discovered that somehow they had 'lost' a few hours. Even so, it is easy enough to be mistaken about the time. But then Betty began to have some extraordinary dreams: she was on board a spacecraft, being examined by extra-terrestrials. Under hypnosis, she recounted the details of the event, saying that this was no dream, but had actually happened during those 'lost' two hours. Many years later she was to produce a star-map, drawn from her memory of one shown to her by the aliens, which she said indicated the star of their origin, Eta Reticuli. This map, in fact, is of no value: *any* pattern of dots can be matched up to the night sky

somewhere, and experiments done with a random-number generator have produced much better representations of the region of Eta Reticuli than Betty's. Yet why should Betty be prompted to draw a star-map?

It is interesting that Barney's experience was somewhat different. Obviously his wife told him about her vivid dreams, and in due course he came to believe that the events depicted therein had actually happened. However, even under hypnosis, he was able to give only the vaguest of details about these assumed events. The psychiatrist who worked with the Hills was convinced that the whole affair was a product solely of Betty's mind.

The most fashionistic view of UFOs today is that they are all the product of people's minds. This is not to say that observers are simply 'seeing things', although obviously a lot of UFO sightings owe their origins to genuine misinterpretations of natural phenomena (ball lightning, distorted views of the planet Venus, and so on). What really happens, say many modern ufologists, is that UFOs are reified – brought into reality – by the right-brains of individual human beings; once reified, the objects can be seen by other people.

LEFT: *Two versions of a photograph taken in October 1981 by Hannah McRoberts to the north of Kelsey Bay, Vancouver Island, British Columbia. Ms McRoberts was simply taking pictures of the mountain, and at the time neither she nor her companions noticed the UFO revealed in the enlargement.*

ABOVE: *A photograph taken in 1966 in New Mexico showing what purports to be a small, remote-controlled flying saucer, about 3ft (1m) in diameter. Photograhs such as this one understandably arouse deep scepticism among modern ufologists.*

This matches well with theories concerning the poltergeist effect (*see* page 44). For example, in 1948 a large glowing object was spotted over Kentucky, and three USAF pilots were sent to investigate. One of them, Thomas Mantell, got very close to the object and over the radio gave graphic descriptions of it. Then his radio transmissions ceased, and some while later the wreckage of his airplane was discovered. What was he chasing? Almost certainly, it was a weather balloon: Mantell, not equipped with oxygen, flew too high and blacked out. Yet the evidence that there were weather balloons in that area is not especially convincing. Moreover, Mantell's two colleagues, who returned safely to base, saw nothing. It is possible that Mantell was chasing a chimera born from his own mind . . . and yet he was investigating the object solely because of prior ground-based observations of it. If the object was a weather balloon, why did the other pilots not see it? If it was the product of someone's right-brain, then whose? Several decades later, we have little chance of solving this particular mystery.

That UFOs are mental, rather than straightforwardly physical, phenomena is a notion supported by the experiences during the later 1970s and early 1980s of the Sunderland family, who lived on the northern Welsh border. The mother and three of her children had many very curious UFO encounters, a few of them while awake, but most of them in dreams. Scientists were totally incapable of explaining the events, except that they were born from the minds of the Sunderlands; yet, in orthodox scientific terms, this hardly explains the waking encounters. It is easy enough

to explain away the children's dramatic dreams as merely a result of an overdose of science-fiction videos, but the same does not apply to encounters *shared by more than one child*. Clearly there was some mental phenomenon at work here which we do not yet fully – or even partially – understand.

The idea that aliens might visit us is, of course, not innately foolish. It seems highly probable that there are many other civilized cultures out there in the universe, although we have no way of knowing quite how rife life, let alone intelligent life, is. During the past couple of decades a great many people have made a great deal of money out of the suggestion that aliens visited us during prehistory and promoted our intellectual development. This is possible, but to date not a single piece of convincing evidence has been produced – whatever they say on the covers of the

LEFT: A single UFO photographed in 1982 at Hessdalen, Norway. As noted on page 105, these lights are believed to be unidentified atmospheric phenomena rather than material objects. **ABOVE:** *A classic fake; note the poor focus.* **RIGHT:** *UFOs photographed at Conisburgh, Yorkshire, in March 1966 by Stephen Pratt, then aged 14. The precise nature of these objects must remain a matter for debate.*

paperbacks! One attractive notion is that life on earth started solely because a visiting spacecraft landed and, as it were, emptied its chemical toilets, complete with microorganisms, which over the billennia evolved to produce human beings. This is a notion much more appealing than the idea that, to take just a single example, Jesus Christ was a visitor from outer space. One's general attitude might be summarized by quoting the opening of Erich von Däniken's seminal work, *Chariots of the Gods?*: 'It took courage to write this book, and it will take courage to read it'.

Is there any possibility, then, that one day we shall encounter an extraterrestrial civilization? Sceptics point to

the fact that we haven't yet; if there are, as the optimists suggest, a million technologically advanced civilizations in our own galaxy, then why have none come to visit us? Various ufologists, of course, assert that indeed they have; but this is unconvincing. The economics of travelling between the stars are frightening – just think of the cost of a single Space Shuttle mission – and so it is unlikely that extraterrestrial civilizations will expend megabucks on cheerful family tourism to a minor planet in the galaxy's backwaters.

There are various possible reasons why extraterrestrials have failed to visit us during historical times. One is that we are the only technological civilization in our corner of the

galaxy, or even in the entire universe. Another is that the distances between the stars are simply too huge for interstellar travel to be a practicable possibility. Yet again, are we not making an anthropocentric assumption in thinking that other civilizations would have the remotest interest in getting in touch with us?

But the real reason why we have heard nothing from the outside universe may be much more prosaic: we haven't been looking. The most famous attempt to pick up radio signals from other civilizations was Project Ozma in 1960: for less than 200 hours two 'probable' nearby stars were the object of attention of radioastronomers at Green Bank. The idea of this experiment was that it should merely demonstrate a principle; yet it was widely derided for its failure to record incoming alien communications. The cynics possibly did not pause to ponder the statistical likelihood that the putative civilizations associated with two stars out of billions would just happen to beam a transmission in our

direction so that it would arrive some time during those eight days. The governments of the developed countries of our world (with the reputed exception of the USSR) have, however, since then unanimously decided to agree with the cynics and not 'waste money' on the search for extraterrestrial intelligence.

A final reason for our lack of contact with the assumed aliens is hardly to be taken seriously, but the theory – the product of Charles Fort's ever-fertile mind – is fun. His idea was that 'we are property' – in other words, the 'cattle' of the universe. Of course, you only bother to visit your cattle when you need to, and so far our owners have not needed to. But there may come a time.

Seeking out UFOs can be a chilly business. This 1984 photograph shows the basecamp for Project Hessdalen, whose task was to investigate the mysterious lights seen there.

LOST LANDS

THE LIST OF REPUTED lost lands – continents, countries or cities that have disappeared or have 'locked themselves away' behind some impenetrable supernatural barrier – is virtually endless. The most famous of all is Atlantis; runners-up are Mu and Lemuria. But lands such as Avalon, Shangri-La and the Gardens of the Hesperides are well known, too. One of particular interest is the city of Troy, long believed to be a myth. Its remains were finally tracked down by Arthur Schliemann in 1870, showing that some tales of lost lands are not as foolish as they may seem. What is not generally known is that this 'mighty city' was in fact the size of the average modern village.

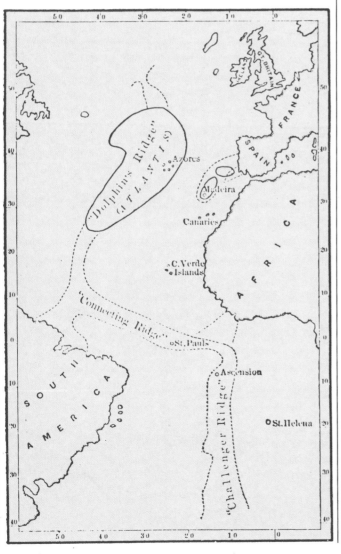

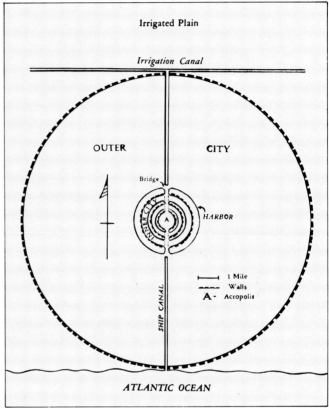

Stories about Atlantis date back to the *Critias* and *Timaeus* of Plato, who lived in the 4th century BC. In these works he put it into the mouths of his characters that Solon had been told by an Egyptian priest that a now-destroyed continent had once existed beyond the Pillars of Hercules (i.e., beyond the mouth of the Mediterranean). Ever since, legends about Atlantis have proliferated, at no time more than during the last century or so.

The 'modern revival' of Atlantology came about because of a remarkable book, published in 1882: *Atlantis, the Antediluvian World*, by the American writer and politician Ignatius Donnelly. Donnelly's work cannot be described as a ripping yarn: it is closely argued, and presents a plethora of

ABOVE: *A hypothetical map of the city of Atlantis, capital of the continent, based on the account in Plato's Critias.* **LEFT:** *Ignatius Donnelly's book, Atlantis the Antediluvian World (1882), was responsible for creating the modern 'cult' of Atlantology. This map shows his estimation of the continent's erstwhile position, based on deep-sea soundings. The ridges marked represent the Mid-Atlantic Ridge, which we now know to be an area where molten rock is emerging from beneath our planet's crust. This renders Donnelly's proposed siting dubious.*

evidence that there did indeed, at one time, exist a continent in the Atlantic Ocean. Zoological, geographical and sociological data are presented at considerable length. The only trouble is that such data are based purely upon hypotheses, and often further hypotheses are based on the original ones. Yet Donnelly's speculations clearly struck a popular chord, because even today new books about Atlantis are being published, each with a more outrageous central theory than the last.

The credulity of otherwise intelligent people cannot be stressed too much. A few years ago, I published a parody called *Sex Secrets of Ancient Atlantis*, and I was startled to receive a couple of letters from readers of the book who requested further information! Even the great are not immune from the Atlantology cult: the 19th-century British prime minister, William Gladstone, was at one stage moved to request funds from the Treasury so that an expedition could be sent to discover the lost continent (his request was refused).

So is there any reality behind the Atlantis legend? It seems that there probably is. In about 1400 BC the Mediterranean island of Thēra (now called Santorini) exploded, Krakatoa-fashion, annihilating the culture then residing on Thēra. More importantly, the tsunami resulting from the explosion seems to have destroyed the highly advanced Minoan civilization, based on the island of Crete. The loss of this culture was a significant event – certainly so far as the ancient world was concerned. Tales get better with the telling, and it seems reasonable to suggest that by Plato's time the lost land had become so huge, according to popular accounts, that it could no longer be 'fitted into' the Mediterranean. Hence, it must lie in the ocean beyond. (It seems likely that Plato used the tale of Atlantis solely for the sake of making philosophical points: there is no evidence that he actually believed it.)

UPPER RIGHT: *Artist's impression of the gardens of the royal palace in Atlantis*
LOWER RIGHT: *the royal banqueting hall*
BELOW: *the Palace of King Agamemnon*

The legend of Lemuria was born from the puzzlement of scientists during the 19th and early 20th centuries about the distribution of lemurs around the Indian Ocean. The first person to suggest that this could be explained in terms of a lost continent – that modern lemurs were the descendants of the lucky ones that had escaped to the shores of nearby land masses – seems to have been the British geologist Philip Lutley Sclater.

It is hard to agree with all of Sclater's ideas – one balks, for example, at his explanation of the suicidal habits of lemmings as an attempt to migrate from Europe to Atlantis – yet his suggestion that there might have been such a continent as Lemuria was at the time perfectly reasonable. Sadly, various occult groups, such as the Theosophists, latched onto the idea and produced various theories whose proofs had less than scientific rigour – for example, that Lemuria was originally populated 18 million years ago by Venusians, who lived there quite happily for a long while before accidentally discovering sex and thereby incurring the destruction of their continent.

The myth of Mu – often confused with Lemuria, because it, too, is supposed to have been in the Indian Ocean – has far less honourable origins. The myth was invented by Augustus Le Plongeon for a book called *Queen Moo and the Egyptian Sphynx*, published in 1896. The book purported to be based on ancient Mayan writings to which Le Plongeon was privy, although strangely enough copies were not available to other investigators. Colonel James Churchward 'took over' the legend of Mu: he published four books on the lost land during the 1920s and 1930s. His purpose was racist: he presented the case that the white races were superior to all others because they were more closely related to the superbeings who had inhabited Mu.

Have there been lost continents? In a sense, yes. The continents of our world have drifted about the face of the globe over the past few billion years, occasionally colliding to form temporary marriages and occasionally divorcing again. Their promiscuity can be explained in terms of the theory of plate tectonics. On occasion the continents have

TOP: *The submersion of Mu; 'Temples and palaces came crashing to the ground.' Or, at least, that was the story according to James Churchward in his book* The Lost Continent of Mu *(1931), from which this illustration has been taken.* **RIGHT:** *An illustration from Jules Verne's* 20,000 Leagues Under the Sea, *showing the French writer's view of the destruction of Atlantis.* **FAR RIGHT:** *'André Laurie' was the pseudonym of Paschal Grousset, a French communist novelist who collaborated on occasion with Verne. His version of Atlantis was, as one might expect, highly politicized.*

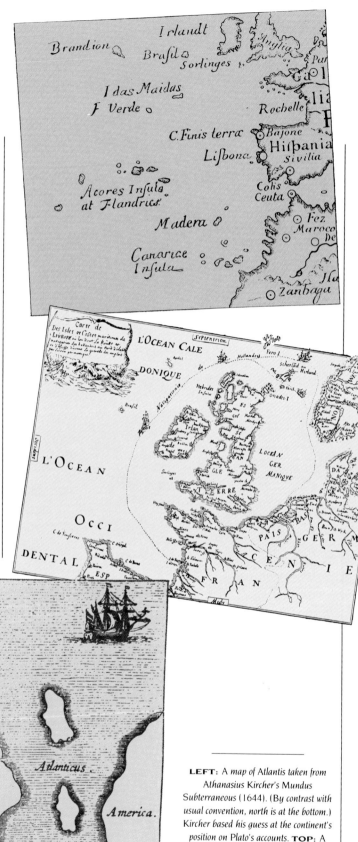

come together to form 'supercontinents'. For example, several hundred million years ago all the continents came together to form a single land mass (now called Pangaea by geologists), which split up to form two supercontinents (Laurasia and Gondwanaland). These in turn split up.

Why is it reasonable to credit the one-time existence of continents such as Laurasia and Gondwanaland, but to reject Atlantis, Lemuria and Mu? The explanation is very simple. There is very good scientific evidence, from a diversity of disciplines, in support of Laurasia and Gondwanaland. There is none whatsoever in favour of Atlantis, Lemuria and Mu – unless the legend of Atlantis is genuinely a corruption of accounts of the destruction of the Minoan civilization.

Concerning Atlantis, there is one further suggestion. Our ancestors were far better navigators than we generally assume. Is it possible that they managed, several centuries before Christ, to reach the Americas? There they could have found various advanced cultures – now, alas, long gone because of the 'civilizing' efforts of the invading Europeans over the past few hundred years.

The discovery of, say, a Phoenician artefact in the Americas would cause something of a sensation in the archaeological world, but it would also destroy a mountain of Atlantological theses overnight.

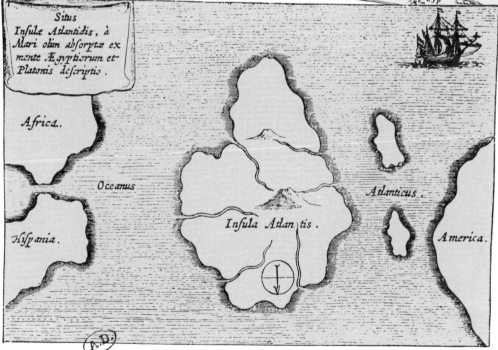

LEFT: A map of Atlantis taken from Athanasius Kircher's Mundus Subterraneous (1644). (By contrast with usual convention, north is at the bottom.) Kircher based his guess at the continent's position on Plato's accounts. **TOP:** A chart from the 1609 book La Navigation l'Inde Oriental, showing the islands of Brasil and Brandion. **ABOVE:** A chart made in 1634 by the French Geographer Royal showing the island of Brasil.

UNORTHODOX COSMOLOGIES

IS THE EARTH HOLLOW? Is the entire universe (the earth and sun excepted) made of ice? Or is the universe a giant brain?

The answer to all three questions can be anticipated, yet there are still educated adults who subscribe to these theories. I once put forward the third of them as a joke in a science-fiction magazine, only to discover later, to my horror, that someone else had published a book that quite seriously presented the case.

There are two quite disparate versions of the idea that the earth is hollow. The first is the simple one: we live on a planet that is nothing more than a superficial crust. The inside of the earth is either a vast cavern or it consists of various concentric spheres, each separated by an air-filled gap – rather as if it were some sort of vast Russian doll. There have been various hypotheses put forward in favour of these notions – such as that UFOs are piloted by malevolent Nazis who escaped at the end of World War II to live inside the hollow earth. To say that the scientific evidence is zero is to understate matters: if the earth were indeed hollow, or even only partly so, the works of Newton and Einstein would have to be rewritten from scratch, because our ideas of gravitation would have to change. Alas, our ideas of gravitation seem to work pretty well.

The second hollow-earth theory is so much at variance with modern science that it is, in a way, more reasonable. It seems first to have been put forward by the 19th-century American mystic Cyrus Reed Teed (who liked to refer to himself as Koresh). The notion is that we live not on the outside of a sphere, but on the *inside* of a sort of spherical bubble in the rock that constitutes the rest of the universe. During World War II the Nazis, who were keen to discredit Einstein – a Jew – temporarily espoused Teed's theory. Infra-red telescopes were on one occasion directed towards the sky in order to spy on the manoeuvres of the British fleet in the English Channel.

The Nazis soon realized that Teed's theories had little going for them. However, they were still eager to find some totally non-Einsteinian cosmology, and so they quarrried the notions of the ideologically sound Hans Hörbiger. He had, as early as 1913, 'discovered' that the stars were not other suns at all, but chunks of ice, comparatively nearby and, like every other body in the universe, in orbit about the sun. However, since space was not a vacuum, but filled with rarefied hydrogen, 'air resistance' caused the orbits of all celestial bodies to decay. They spiralled in towards the sun and finally impacted, producing a sunspot. When this happened to a star, its ice was, obviously, vaporized and blasted spacewards; some of this vapour reached the upper atmosphere of the earth, where it recrystallized to form high-altitude clouds.

The world (or cosmic) ice theory may seem hilarious to us now, but it was not quite so funny for German physicists in the 1930s, whose lectures were disrupted by pro-Nazi students chanting that they wanted Hörbiger, not Einstein, and who threatened and often carried out physical violence. Even after the Nazi insanity, Hörbiger's ideas (of which only a few have been summarized here) had a cult following throughout much of the Western world. It was to be some decades later before even the most diehard enthusiasts lost heart. Why? Well, consider this sentence from a 1953 pamphlet produced by the Hörbiger Institute: 'The final proof of the whole cosmic ice theory will be obtained when the first landing on the ice-coated surface of the Moon takes place'.

What, then, of the universe as a giant brain? This notion has been put forward by David Foster in his book, *The Intelligent Universe* (1975). He notes the startling similarities between the universe and a giant electronic computer. For example, computers store and process data in the form of 'bits', whereas the universe stores and processes data in the form of subatomic particles, which can be considered as analogous to 'bits'.

Unorthodox cosmologies are legion, as are unorthodox cosmologists. It is easy enough to make a mockery of these people and their theories, and in truth most of them thoroughly deserve it. Yet we have to be careful. Early in this century Alfred Wegener, in an attempt to explain various geological and paleontological phenomena, suggested that the continents drifted around the face of the globe. He was subjected to some of the vilest ridicule from the scientific establishment, and yet now, long after his death, continental drift is almost universally accepted. And think of some of the abuse to which Darwin and Wallace were subjected when they proposed the evolution of living organisms through natural selection.

Scientific advance can come about only through the courage of individuals to stick their necks out. Such individuals need not necessarily be qualified – look at the contributions made by the untrained Peter Wright to the technological achievements of Britain's security services.

Wegener was qualified in many scientific fields, but not in geology or paleontology, which was why he suffered such a torrent of abuse. Of course, one has to draw a line somewhere – the cosmological ideas of Immanuel Velikovsky spring instantly to mind – yet we should not too enthusiastically discard the ideas of the unorthodox cosmologists. Just a few of them against all the probabilities, and in the face of all scepticism and doubt, might be right.

This is a matter of much importance when discussing mysteries. Most of the phenomena and ideas we have been discussing in this book are such that, if even a single one were correct, much of orthodox science would have to be rewritten. What happens to zoology if the Loch Ness Monster is finally tracked down? What happens to physics and psychology the first time someone is *proved* to be capable of psychokinesis? What happens to the theory of relativity if it can be proved beyond doubt that someone has

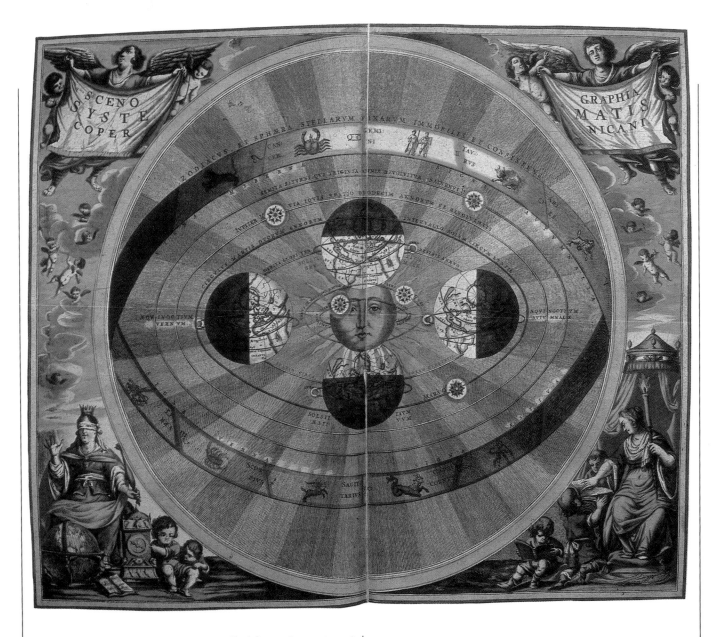

— either mentally or physically — travelled through time? And what happens to our world-view should reincarnation be established as an irrefutable fact?

All of these things are currently mysteries, because we cannot completely explain them. Tomorrow — or next year, or in the next century — we may radically have to revise our ideas in the light of new knowledge. Today's unorthodox cosmologies and our notions about the paranormal may one day be part of accepted knowledge, and our current scientific theories may be shown to be so ridiculous that they themselves become unorthodox cosmologies — presumably with minor cult followings.

Remember, once upon a time it was known for certain that the earth was flat.

It is always worth remembering that today's unorthodox cosmology sometimes becomes tomorrow's accepted fact. For centuries the Ptolemaic view of the universe **LEFT** *held sway. This had the earth at the centre of all creation, with the moon, sun, planets and stars travelling around it in their different spheres. Generally it was believed that the earth was flat, despite the fact that ancient Greek philosophers such as Aristotle and Eratosthenes had proved it to be a ball and even calculated its diameter. Mariners must have known, through observation, that the Ptolemaic Theory was nonsensical, yet they continued to use it because it gave suitably accurate results for navigation use. By the 16th century, however, dissent concerning the theory was growing among the intellectual community. In 1543 Copernicus, on his death bed, published his theory that the earth and the other planets orbited the sun* **ABOVE.** *His ideas were attacked by both religious and scientific authorities, but within decades had become generally accepted. It is hard to believe that some of the wilder theories in circulation today bear any truth.*

BIBLIOGRAPHY

THIS BIBLIOGRAPHY IS A selective one. Even so, not all the books listed can be regarded as 'recommended reading'. Some are, to put it bluntly . . . but no, we cannot put it quite that bluntly. Editions cited are those used, and may not necessarily be the first. Editions marked * have inadequate indexes; those marked ** have no index at all.

Ashe, Geoffrey, *The Ancient Wisdom*, London, Macmillan, 1977

Ashe, Geoffrey, *King Arthur's Avalon*, London, Collins, 1957

Begg, Paul, *Into Thin Air*, Newton Abbot, David & Charles, 1979

** Berlitz, Charles, *Mysteries From Forgotten Worlds*, London, Souvenir, 1972

** Berlitz, Charles, *The Mystery of Atlantis*, London, Souvenir, 1976

Bernstein, Morey: *The Search for Bridey Murphy*, London, Hutchinson, 1956

Brookesmith, Peter (ed.,), *The Alien World*, London, Orbis, 1984

* Buck, Alice E, and Palmer, F Claude, *The Clothes of God*, London, Peter Owen, 1956

** Caldwell, Taylor, with Stearn, Jess, *The Romance of Atlantis*, London, Severn House, 1977

** Cathie, Bruce, *The Pulse of the Universe: Harmonic 288*, London, Sphere, 1981

Cavendish, Richard, *A History of Magic*, London, Weidenfeld & Nicholson, 1977

Cavendish, Richard, *Unsolved Mysteries of the Universe*, London, Treasure Press, 1987

* Cavendish, Richard (ed.), *Encyclopedia of the Un-explained*, London, Routledge & Kegan Paul, 1974

** Charroux, Robert, *The Mysterious Unknown*, London, Spearman, 1972

Cochrane, Hugh H, *Gateway to Oblivion*, London, Star, 1981

* Costello, Peter, *The Magic Zoo*, London, Sphere, 1979

Cramer, Marc, *The Devil Within*, London, W. H. Allen, 1979

Dunne, J W, *An Experiment with Time* (5th edn.), London, Faber, 1939

Edelson, Edward, *Who Goes There?*, London, New English Library, 1980

* Evans, Christopher, *Cults of Unreason*, London, Harrap, 1973

* Eysenck, Hans J, and Sargent, Carl, *Explaining the Unexplained*, London, Weidenfeld & Nicholson, 1982

** Fort, Charles, *The Book of the Damned*, London, Abacus, 1973

Foster, David, *The Intelligent Universe*, London, Abelard-Schuman, 1975

** Gibson, Walter B, and Gibson, Litzka R, *The Encyclo-paedia of Prophecy*, London, Granada, 1977

Goldsmith, Donald, and Owen, Tobias, *The Search for Life in the Universe*, Menlo Park (Cal), Benjamin/Cummings, 1980

Gooch, Stan, *The Paranormal*, London, Wildwood, 1978

Goss, Michael, *The Evidence for Phantom Hitch-hikers*, Wellingborough, Aquarian Press, 1984

** Grant, Douglas, *The Cock Lane Ghost*, London, Macmillan, 1965

** Grant, Joan, *Winged Pharaoh*, London, Arthur Barker, 1937 (novel)

Grant, John, *A Directory of Discarded Ideas*, Sevenoaks, Ashgrove Press, 1981

Grant, John, *Dreamers*, Bath, Ashgrove Press, 1984

Grant, John, 'The Flight of Reason', *Common Ground*, November 1981

Grant, John, 'Not Such a Tippe-top Idea', *Common Ground*, May 1982

Grant, John, *Sex Secrets of Ancient Atlantis*, London, Grafton, 1985

Grant, John, 'Things That Go Crank in the Night', *Common Ground*, February 1982

* Grant, John (ed.), *The Book of Time* (Consultant Editor Colin Wilson), Newton Abbot, Westbridge, 1980

** Greene, Graham, *A Sort of Life*, London, Bodley Head, 1971

Gribbin, John, *Timewarps*, London, Dent, 1979

Gurney, Edmund, Myers, Frederic W H, and Podmore, Frank, *Phantasms of the Living*, London, Society for Psychical Research and Trübner, 1886

** Harrison, Michael, *Vanishings*, London, New English Library, 1981

Heuvelmans, Bernard, *In the Wake of the Sea-Serpents*, London, Rupert Hart-Davis, 1968 (trans.)

Heuvelmans, Bernard, *On the Track of Unknown Animals*, London, Paladin, 1970 (abridged trans.)

* Koestler, Arthur, *The Roots of Coincidence*, London, Hutchinson, 1972

Kolosimo, Peter, *Timeless Earth*, London, Sphere, 1974 (trans.)

Krupp, E C (ed.), *In Search of Ancient Astronomies*, London, Chatto & Windus, 1980

** Landsburg, Alan, *In Search of Myths and Monsters*, London, Corgi, 1977

Leonard, George H, *Someone Else is on Our Moon*, London, W H Allen, 1977

** Leslie, Desmond, and Adamski, George, *Flying Saucers Have Landed*, London, Futura, 1977

** Loosley, William Robert, *An Account of a Meeting with Denizens of Another World, 1871*, 'edited' by David Langford, Newton Abbot, David & Charles, 1979

* McClure, Kevin, *The Evidence for Visions of the Virgin Mary*, Aquarian Press, Wellingborough, 1983

** McConnell, Brian, and Bence, Douglas, *The Nilsen File*, London, Futura, 1983

Mackal, Roy P, *The Monsters of Loch Ness*, London, Futura, 1976

Maple, Eric, *The Realm of Ghosts*, London, Hale, 1964

Masters, Anthony, *The Natural History of the Vampire*, London, Granada, 1974

Mavor, James W, *Voyage to Atlantis*, London, Souvenir, 1969

Menzel, Donald H, and Taves, Ernest H, *The UFO Enigma*, Garden City (NJ), Doubleday, 1977

Michell, John, and Rickard, Robert J M, *Phenomena*, London, Thames & Hudson, 1977

Moore, Patrick, *Can You Speak Venusian?*, Newton Abbot, David & Charles, 1972

Morgan, Chris, and Langford, David, *Facts and Fallacies*, Exeter, Webb & Bower, 1981

Napier, John, *Bigfoot*, London, Cape, 1972

Nash, Jay Robert, *Compendium of World Crime*, London, Harrap, 1983 (originally published in the United States as *Almanac of World Crime*, 1981)

Noorbergen, Rene, *Secrets of the Lost Races*, London, New English Library, 1978

* Panati, Charles, *Supersenses*, London, Cape, 1975

* Pedler, Kit, *Mind Over Matter*, London, Eyre Methuen, 1981

Permutt, Cyril, *Beyond the Spectrum*, Cambridge, Patrick Stephens, 1983

Playfair, Guy Lyon, *The Indefinite Boundary*, London, Souvenir, 1976

Playfair, Guy Lyon, *The Unknown Power*, London, Granada, 1977 (originally published as *The Flying Cow*)

Randles, Jenny, *The Pennine UFO Mystery*, London, Grafton, 1983

Randles, Jenny, and Whetnall, Paul, *Alien Contact*, London, Coronet, 1983

** Sachs, Margaret, *The UFO Encyclopedia*, London, Corgi, 1981

Sassoon, George, and Dale, Rodney, *The Manna Machine*, London, Sidgwick & Jackson, 1978

Sladek, John, *The New Apocrypha*, London, Hart-Davis MacGibbon, 1974

** Smith, Adam, *Powers of Mind*, London, W H Allen, 1976

Stoneley, Jack, and Lawton, A T, *CETI*, London, Star, 1976

* Stoneley, Jack, and Lawton, A T, *Is Anyone Out There?*, London, Star, 1975

** Stoneley, Jack, and Lawton, A T, *Tunguska: Cauldron of Hell*, London, Star, 1977

Story, Ronald, *Guardians of the Universe*, London, New English Library, 1980

Story, Ronald, *The Space-Gods Revealed*, London, New English Library, 1978

Vaughan, Alan, *Patterns of Prophecy*, London, Turnstone, 1974

* von Däniken, Erich, *Chariots of the Gods?*, London, Souvenir, 1969 (trans.)

** Waring, Philippa, *A Dictionary of Omens and Superstitions*, London, Souvenir, 1978

Warshofsky, Fred, *Doomsday*, London, Sphere, 1979

Watson, Lyall, *Lifetide*, London, Hodder & Stoughton, 1979

Watson, Lyall, *Supernature*, London, Hodder & Stoughton, 1973

** Watson, Peter, *Twins*, London, Hutchinson, 1981

* Webb, James, *The Occult Establishment*, Glasgow, Richard Drew, 1981

** Wellard, James, *The Search for Lost Worlds*, London, Pan, 1975

Wilson, Colin, *A Criminal History of Mankind*, London, Granada, 1984

Wilson, Colin, *Mysteries*, London, Hodder & Stoughton, 1978

Wilson, Colin, *Poltergeist!*, London, New English Library, 1981

Wilson, Colin, and Grant, John (eds.), *The Directory of Possibilities*, Exeter, Webb & Bower, 1981

* Wright, Peter, and Greengrass, Paul, *Spycatcher*, New York, Viking, 1987

INDEX

PICTURE CREDITS